Is There
A Synoptic
Problem?

Is There
A Synoptic
Problem?

*Rethinking the Literary Dependence
of the First Three Gospels*

Eta Linnemann

Translated from the German edition,
Gibt es ein synoptisches Problem?
by Robert W. Yarbrough

BAKER BOOK HOUSE
Grand Rapids, Michigan 49516

Library of Congress Cataloging-in-Publication Data

Linnemann, Eta.
  [Gibt es ein synoptisches problem? English]
  Is there a synoptic problem? : rethinking the literary dependence of the
first three gospels / Eta Linnemann ; translated from the German by
Robert W. Yarbrough.
     p.   cm.
  Translation of : Gibt es ein synoptisches problem?
  Includes bibliographical references and index.
  1. Synoptic problem. 2. Bible N.T. Gospels—Criticism, interpretation,
etc. I. Title.
  BS2555.2.L5613 1992
  226'.066—dc20   92-8555

Originally published in German under the title *Gibt es ein synoptisches Problem?*
by Eta Linnemann. Published by Hänssler-Verlag (Friedrich Hänssler KG, Bis-
marckstr. 4, D-7303 Neuhausen, Germany, 1992). All rights reserved.

Footnotes in brackets ([ ]) indicate material added by the translator for clarification.

Contents

Introduction   9

Part 1   How Scientific Is Scientific Theology?

1 Theological Science as Research—a Historical Review   19
2 New Testament Criticism in Academic Studies   43

Part 2   Is There Literary Dependence among the Synoptic Gospels?

Introduction to Part 2   67
3 The Composition of Matthew and Luke   75
4 Commonality in the Narrative Thread of the Synoptic Gospels   83
5 The Extent of Parallelism Between Matthew, Mark, and Luke: A Longitudinal Investigation   97
6 Quantitative Synoptic Comparison: A Representative Cross-Section   109
7 The Significance of the Extent of Similarities in Vocabulary   131
8 The Probability of Literary Dependence   145

Part 3   Could the Synoptic Gospels Have Arisen Independently?

9 The Possibility of Understanding the Synoptic Gospels Without Literary Dependence   155
10 The Origin of the Synoptic Gospels   177

Part 4   Why Four Gospels?

11 The Purpose of the Four Gospels   195
12 The Treatment of the Four Gospels   205
Epilog   209
Bibliography   211
Index   213

"Gibt es einen Menschen, der so leichtgläubig ist wie der,

welcher nicht an die Bibel glauben will?

Er verschluckt eine Tonne von Schwierigkeiten, während er sich beklagt,

daß wir ein Gramm davon verschluckt haben."

C. H. Spurgeon[1]

"Is anyone so gullible as the person
who determines not to believe the Bible?
He swallows a ton of difficulties, while complaining
that we have swallowed an ounce."

1. *Auf Dein Wort. Andachten für jeden Tag*, 2d ed. (CLV Bielefeld, 1986), 50.

Acknowledgements

I thank those whose prayers gave rise to and have accompanied this book, especially my prayer circle under the leadership of Brother Werner Heyen; my sisters in Christ, Else Piel and Doris Radsiek, and Elisabeth Hettinger's prayer circle. I also thank Veronika Elbers, who prayed daily that I would again get down to work at my desk.

My thanks also go to those who strengthened and encouraged me as I researched and wrote: Brother Hans-Peter Grabe, Brother Gerhard Ulrichs, Dr. Klaus Sensche, and Gundula Weber.

I am grateful to Hänssler-Verlag, the German publisher who, without hesitation, agreed to bring the book out—even before I had finished writing. My thanks also go to Baker Book House for their speedy production of the English-language edition. Allan Fisher, Jim Weaver, and Paul Ingram merit special mention for their efficiency and diligence. Dan Malda, director of design and typesetting, achieved enviable results in the task of creating readable charts. His patience was remarkable. Robert Yarbrough, Covenant Theological Seminary, has kindly sacrificed time from his own writing to furnish the translation.

While many deserve thanks, all honor belongs to God alone, who led me to this project and then gave me wisdom and strength to complete it. Trusting in him, I venture to publish these findings, vulnerable to criticism though they be, so that they may be of service to many as quickly as possible.

Eta Linnemann
Leer-Loga, Germany
February 13, 1991

Introduction

Professor Eta Linnemann was formerly an internationally recognized practitioner of what she now calls "historical-critical theology." Her book *Historical Criticism of the Bible: Methodology or Ideology?* (Grand Rapids: Baker, 1990) explains why she came to reject this school of biblical scholarship and the dangers she sees as inherent in its continuing impact on worldwide theological education.

In the interview that follows she answers questions frequently asked of her since she left her university post in Germany to become a Bible teacher and scholar in her native Germany, Indonesia, and other lands. Her answers introduce the topic of this book.

Question: Have you never regretted breaking with theological science, especially now that you are instructing students again in Batu, Indonesia?

Eta Linnemann: If by theological science you mean historical-critical theology, absolutely not! As time passes, I become more and more convinced that to a considerable degree New Testament criticism as practiced by those committed to historical-critical theology does not deserve to be called science.

Question: Could you give an example of what you are talking about?

E. L.: Let's take the so-called "Synoptic problem," which asserts the following: "The similarities and differences between the Gospels of Matthew, Mark, and Luke present a problem. This problem can only be unraveled by assuming a literary relationship among them. The various authors must have copied from each other or consulted the same written sources or both."

The solution to the Synoptic problem is the cornerstone of New Testament criticism. Remove it, and both form criticism and redaction criticism also collapse. I am shocked when I look at the books of my former colleagues, which I used to hold in highest esteem, and examine the justification for their position. Instead of proof I find only assertions. Instead of arguments there is merely circular reasoning.

Question: Is there actually no proof for a literary relationship among the Gospels?

E. L.: It is assumed from the outset that literary dependence exists. Other possibilities receive no consideration, or are groundlessly opposed with the accusation that they are "uncritical." From the outset the student is not exposed to the facts but is presented with four hypotheses from which to choose: (1) the Gospels all stem from a proto-gospel, a single original gospel no longer in existence; (2) the Gospels stem from an earlier collection of writings; (3) the Gospels owe their existence to various oral traditions that comprised a proto-gospel; (4) the Gospels are the result of interdependence among the Synoptic writers. The fourth hypothesis receives special emphasis.

The alleged literary dependence is not proven. The star witness for the claim that Matthew and Luke show literary dependence is Karl Lachmann [1793–1851], although he maintained that "it is obvious that they [Matthew and Luke] did not copy from the Gospel of Mark." Individual passages are grasped at to demonstrate the literary dependence. These come, as a rule, from words of Jesus where, as a matter of fact, the literal agreement among the Gospels runs close to 100 percent.

What the student never hears is this: There are more likely and plausible explanations for these agreements than the assumption of literary dependence.

Question: What did you mean when you mentioned circular reasoning?

E. L.: One begins arguing by assuming the validity of the hypothesis that the argument will attempt to prove. In response to the many facts that weigh against this assumption, one immediately comes up with secondary explanations. These not only assume what they are supposed to prove; they also are set forth as established facts: "Matthew and Luke make improvements in many places." "Matthew smoothes . . . introduces words he prefers . . . makes vocabulary improvements." "The variations are—in Luke's thinking—improvements." Where linguistic variations are apparent, these are treated as improvements. Where word order is divergent, this is alleged to confirm "material alteration of the text of Mark by Matthew and Luke." The claim is even made that Matthew and Luke handled Mark "critically"—without any conclusive proof ever being advanced that Matthew and Luke copied from Mark.

Question: But that can't be standard practice!

E. L.: Regrettably, I am not referring to any exceptional occurrence. This is the way things stand across the board in any "introduction" text used today by students. True, the authors of these works are highly intelligent, as well as personally honest, pious, hard-working, and zealous in the work they do to "render a service to God." Nevertheless, they operate within the confines of historical-critical theology, which from the outset sets the opinion of philosophers above God's Word.

Question: But isn't the Synoptic problem, along with its solution, the "two-source" theory, one of the long-established certainties of New Testament criticism?

E. L.: As improbable as it sounds, to this very day, historical-critical theology has never produced an impartial investigation of whether a literary dependence exists, be it direct or indirect, among the Gospels of Matthew, Mark, and Luke—or whether these three Gospels are three equally original reports.

Question: What is the basis for the conviction that literary dependence is a settled fact?

E. L.: Since Gotthold E. Lessing [1729–1781] penned his presumptions on the origin of these Gospels,[1] the view that they are eyewitness reports, or are based on eyewitness reports, has been groundlessly discriminated against—although this is the only view that does justice to the claims of the Gospels about themselves as well as to ancient church tradition.

In addition, although he suppressed the fact, Lessing was an avowed enemy of the Christian faith. In his own words, he set himself the goal of destroying "this hateful edifice of nonsense . . . on the pretense of furnishing new bases for it." Precisely with Lessing, as historical-criticial theology sees it, one can speak of the start of an actual investigation of the Synoptic problem—yet his investigation consisted of nothing more than the construction of hypotheses.

Hypotheses, i.e. assumptions, are the beginning and the foundation of so-called "New Testament criticism," which claims that it conducts actual investigation! Anyone who declined to play along with this game of hypothesis building, preferring instead to ground his thinking in the clear and reliable Word of God, was denounced as unscientific. This tactic made it possible to avoid the bother of conducting an unbiased examination of the facts of the matter, something we normally associate with the concept of science.

Question: Are you saying that there still has been no thorough investigation of the Gospels?

E. L.: I do not wish to be misunderstood: The number of commentaries on the Gospels is legion. Yet, as a rule, they proceed on the basis of a preformed notion regarding the relationships between the Synoptic Gospels and the interpretation of individual passages. Accordingly, they furnish "explanations" for the similarities and differences between the Gospel they interpret and the other two Synoptic Gospels. In the rare case where the connection of one Synoptic with the other two is not

1. Lessing's groundbreaking "Neue Hypothese über die Evangelisten, als bloß menschliche Geschichtsschreiber betrachtet," (1st ed., 1784), appears in *Lessings Werke*, R. Gosche, ed., vol. 7 (Berlin: G. Grote, 1882), 506–26; E.T.: "New Hypotheses concerning the Evangelists regarded as merely human Historians," *Lessing's Theological Writings*, trans. Henry Chadwick (Stanford, Calif.: Stanford University Press, 1957), 65–81.

explicitly explored, the question is not answered but rather is excluded from consideration—the two-source theory being assumed as fact.

Question: Has no one undertaken to investigate the Gospels using computers?

E. L.: On the contrary, that has already been tried a number of times. But the presence of a literary relationship between the Gospels was presupposed from the outset, and the results have reflected this presupposition. In any case, such attempts have not confirmed the claim that the two-source hypothesis offers by far the best solution to the Synoptic problem. For, depending on which study one consults, they arrive at the possibility of three, five, seven, or more interdependent sources. Or they even move the other way and exclude direct literary dependence among the Synoptics.

Now when a half-dozen or more hypotheses can be advanced equally as well-justified solutions to a problem, none of them can claim to be the solution for the problem.

The computer investigations merely confirm what can be shown using other means: The attempt to ground New Testament criticism—a discipline which regards its subject matter only "critically"—on the identification and proposed solutions to the "Synoptic problem" has turned out to be fatefully misguided. From now on it should be recognized that we have arrived at a dead end, similar to the long-obsolete documentary theories that were once used to explain the Pentateuch.[2] It is high time that this be recognized and conceded.

Question: What consequences have these findings had in New Testament scholarhip to date?

E. L.: At the international level scholars still vigorously test hypotheses. In Germany the accepted view is still that the two-source theory is the most viable. But a thorough investigation of the following question is still lacking: "Do the data in the first three Gospels necessitate the acceptance of a literary relationship, or can they be explained just as plausibly as the differences among eyewitnesses?" To date there has been a far too

---

2. For a discussion of how the Graf-Wellhausen theories developed, see Linnemann, *Historical Criticism of the Bible*, 130–37.

naive tendency to chalk up the agreement in content among the Gospels to literary dependence.

Question: Have you already worked on this issue?

E. L.: Yes. In order to determine the extent of the "agreements right down to word order and sentence structure" assumed by those who argue for literary dependence, I have investigated, among other things, a representative cross-section of Mark's Gospel, along with its parallels. This cross-section comprises 34.83 percent of the literary data that Mark contains. At least one pericope as been selected from every chapter; in most instances several have been examined. All of the genres or literary categories postulated by form criticism have been included.

This quantitative Synoptic comparison (in which mere agreement in content is not taken into acount) had the following results: In the cross section examined, just 22.19 percent of the words in parallel passages are completely identical; on the average, given 100 words in Mark, Matthew will have 95.68 differences and Luke 100.43. This means that the verbal similarities are comparatively small and extend chiefly to identical accounts of Jesus' words and to specific and unalterable vocabularly that is required by the nature of what is being related.

These data are quite normal if one assumes the original and independent free formulation of the same events and circumstances. The same data furnish no basis for assuming literary dependence. This conclusion will be confirmed through extensive investigations.

Question: But is this whole issue really of any importance for Christians?

E. L.: I cannot demonstrate the full extent of its significance here, but it is clear that the way the Gospels are generally handled undermines trust in God's Word.

First, hypotheses that assume literary borrowing have the effect of placing the borrower at a temporal distance from the events he relates.

Second, the three-fold witness of the Synoptics is reduced to one when it is concluded, based on the supposed dependence of Matthew and Luke on written sources, that Matthew and

Luke do not contain eyewitness testimony of what they say happened.

Third, if the Synoptics are three reports having a common basis in the reported event, then the differences in parallel passages amount to nothing more than the perspectival contrasts that one would expect when eyewitnesses are involved. Minor discrepancies are normal; supplementary verses can be regarded as additional information. On the other hand, if one assumes dependence on a literary exemplar, then every sentence becomes more or less a falsification of what was originally stated. Then one is required to see Matthew and Luke as the result of arbitrary reworking of the Marcan original.

Fourth, two corollaries follow from the assumption that Matthew and Luke proceeded in such a high-handed manner. One ascribes the use of a similar procedure to Mark. Also, historical-critical theology justifies its own rough handling of God's Word.

Fifth, the authority of God's Word is undermined by the systematic exercise of a critical predisposition to reduce the Word of God to literary-theological construction, instead of seeing it as the revelation of our creator and redeemer.

There are, therefore, good reasons to abandon the gullible acceptance of theology's so-called scientific results instead of taking them as established facts. For we should "no longer be infants, tossed back and forth by the waves, and blown here and there by every wind of teaching and by the cunning and craftiness of men in their deceitful scheming." Let us rather be truthful in love, so that "we will in all things grow up into him who is the Head, that is, Christ" (Eph. 4:14–15).

Part 1

How Scientific
Is Scientific Theology?

1

Theological Science as Research—A Historical Review

The Origin of Theological Science

We are accustomed to viewing theological science as a thorough, well-informed enterprise that stands committed to its subject matter, the Holy Scripture. The fact is, however, quite the reverse: Scientific theology was born, not because people were committed to the Bible, but because they sought reasons to avoid obligation to its teachings.

Even a cursory glance at the sources of biblical criticism shows why scientific theology began in skepticism rather than science. Of the seven key advocates in biblical criticism at its inception—Hugo Grotius (1583–1645), Immanuel Kant (1724–1804), Hermann Reimarus (1694–1768), Johann Semler (1725–1791), Benedict Spinoza (1632–1677), Matthew Tindal (1656–1733), and John Toland (1670–1722)—only Semler was a theologian. The proportion becomes even more unbalanced when one takes into consideration the names of three other philosophers who doubtless merit inclusion in this list, Francis Bacon (1561–1626), Thomas Hobbes (1588–1679), and David Hume (1711–1776).

Since most of these leaders were philosophers, philosophy furnished the fundamental components for biblical criticism.

To a great extent the sacrificial, painstaking labor that scientific theology expends amounts to a working out in intricate detail the philosophical mold into which Scripture must be shaped. Basic philosophical principles, which have been established without reference to the Bible, must be harmonized with the actual biblical data. This, of course, leads to a Sisyphean ordeal, a never-ending and fruitless undertaking.

Scientific biblical exegesis, for the most part, still follows guidelines drawn up by philosophers. All that theologians have carefully watered and nurtured came from seed sown by philosophers—seed that choked out the good seed of the word of God.

By virtue of its very starting point, then, scientific theology lacks any means to engage its subject in an objective manner. Theology and its parent philosophy constitute rather a hostile move to dominate it. They attempt this by posing questions and adopting points of view that have sprung from the soil of a thoroughly conscious and explicitly anti-Christian attitude. The so-called scientific theology has undergone the well-known psychological reaction of "identifying with the attacker."

God's Word has warned us: "See to it that no one takes you captive through hollow and deceptive philosophy, which depends on human tradition and the basic principles of this world rather than on Christ" (Col. 2:8). But we have not heeded the warning. God's Word has admonished us "to contend for the faith that was once for all entrusted to the saints" (Jude 3). But we have heaped insults and scorn on the few who have risked this. God's word has taught us: "Anyone who runs ahead and does not continue in the teaching of Christ does not have God; whoever continues in the teaching has both the Father and the Son. If anyone comes to you and does not bring this teaching, do not take him into your house or welcome him. Anyone who welcomes him shares in his wicked work" (2 John 9–11).

We, however, have welcomed such persons into the best rooms of our theological house and humbly followed their directives.

The Structure of Theological Science[1]

We are accustomed to viewing science as the institutionaliza-tion of certain processes through which, by means of rigorous methodological care and consideration of all relevant points of view, truth is conveyed. Instead, science turns out to be a seduc-tive system of self-realization and reciprocal confirmation.

This state of affairs is presented in an especially clear fashion in Samuel R. Külling's *On the Dating of the 'P' Source in Genesis.*[2]

The late-dating of the so-called priestly writing is, in the words of the theory's mastermind, E. Reuss (1804–1891), "the product of intuition."[3] Reuss passes on this intuition immediately to his students in the easily remembered statement: "The prophets are earlier than the law, and the Psalms more recent than both."[4]

Before there was even an attempt to furnish proof, a student of Reuss named K. H. Graf internalizes this formula, which from then on determines his view of the history of Israel.[5] *That occurs, not through an unimportant detail of scientific work, but through a revolutionary overturning of formerly held viewpoints.* At stake here was the question, in Reuss' own words, "whether we ought to view the history of Israel as standing on its feet or on its head."[6]

Warned in advance by his teacher Reuss of the consequences of this "finding," the disciple Graf at first places it on the back burner. Nevertheless, without being expressly propagated, its ef-fects are perceptible as a background assumption in the books he authors.[7]

Although there had not been even an attempt to furnish sci-entific proof—because even Reuss, the teacher, had contented himself with vague suggestions to avoid difficulties—the disciple Graf writes to Reuss, "I am totally convinced that the entire mid-dle portion of the Pentateuch is post-exilic."[8]

---

1. Part of this section appeared in Eta Linnemann, *Historical Criticism of the Bible* (Grand Rapids: Baker, 1990), 130–34.
2. Samuel R. Külling, *Zur Datierung der 'Genesis-P-Stücke'* (2d ed., Riehen, 1985).
3. Ibid., 5.
4. Ibid.
5. Ibid., 5; see also 7.
6. Ibid., 5.
7. Ibid., 7.
8. Ibid.

This sort of being "totally convinced," which is quite common in the area of "scientific" work, requires no furnishing of proof. It draws from entirely different sources.

This is clearly seen in Graf's case: a review and an article which attempt to question his position serve only to confirm him all the more in his views. This confirmation comes, not through objective disputation in which he weighs opposing arguments, but through a decision.[9]

The "finding" that was passed from teacher to disciple is then interwoven with the views of colleagues and thereby gains a broader basis.[10] Various methodological starting points are employed, and the basic idea takes shape in varying clusters of questions. A process of reciprocal corroboration sets in, and a coalition forms, composed of those who support the basic idea with their own thoughts. Even criticism no longer succeeds in hindering the process now in motion.[11]

In this process there is an striking absence of proof. Külling states, "In the history we have sketched of the exilic/post-exilic dating of the 'P' source in Genesis, we seek in vain for arguments supporting its late dating. In 1869, the 'P' portions were assigned to the exilic/post-exilic era with one fell swoop based on literary-analytical grounds."[12]

Not until later are arguments brought out to undergird the thesis— and then they do not deserve to be called "arguments," for they consist entirely of unproven assertions and judgments based on personal taste.[13]

The movement set in motion by Reuss' "intuition" regarding the dating of the books of the Old Testament finally came to rest when this "intuition" became part of Julius Wellhausen's conception of the history of Israel in his now-famous *Prolegomena to the History of Ancient Israel* (1878). Concerning this book Külling writes:

"The appeal of an entirely new overall picture [of Israel's history], which this work contains, lent to that hypothesis an importance

9. Ibid., 11.
10. Ibid., 10ff., regarding Graf and Kuenen; 11ff. and 21–42, regarding Graf and Hupfeld.
11. Ibid., 36–37.
12. Ibid., 43.
13. Cf. ibid., 44–57.

that was instantly almost overwhelming." [. . .] Wellhausen's historical reconstruction forms the crown of his assignment of a post-exilic origin to P. Wellhausen presents here the consequences of this post-exilic dating of P for the interpretation of the Old Testament in its entirety. [. . .]

Even if we find here no essentially new arguments for the post-exilic dating of P, it is still true that Wellhausen gains a great number of adherents who from now on regard "P" as the latest of the sources[. . .] . He does this through his "masterful connecting of various preliminary studies to form a brilliant and self-contained overall picture." [. . .] [14]

At the outset there was the intuition, at the end the conception, and then the tradition follows; students must learn the conception by heart as a "scientific result." On this they must build, and with it they must work.

In the process that leads from intuition to conception, argumentation also has a place. However, it never serves to furnish proof in the strict sense; important decisions are settled apart from argumentation.

To a limited extent there also remains a place for renewed argumentation as the tradition advances. This argumentation may in some cases even result in certain corrections being made. However, these corrections can no longer call the conception into question in a fundamental way. For the conception, to the extent that it has been accepted, is built into the entire structure of the scientific discipline. Argumentation has only the character of making minor adjustments in the course leading to the final destination of "scientific progress." This destination in itself leads to further strengthening of the conception.

A few conceptions arise independently of others. Most, however, build on earlier conceptions and depend on those foundations, entirely or in part, for support. Some are constructed for the sole purpose of stabilizing earlier, fringe conceptions. Others plug gaps. Still others lead from, or make corrections in, earlier positions. The construction, which in the early stages was loose, becomes increasingly tightly knit together and closed. Views on the outside, which are not interlocked with accepted conceptions (shown in Fig. 1.2 by segment 35), perish.

14. Ibid., 57.

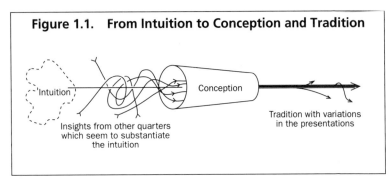

Figure 1.1.   From Intuition to Conception and Tradition

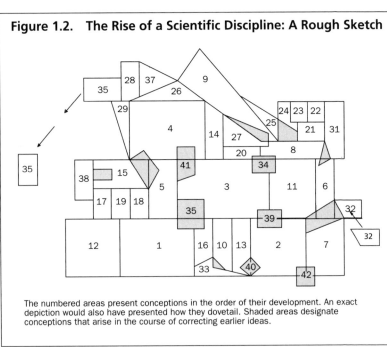

Figure 1.2.   The Rise of a Scientific Discipline: A Rough Sketch

The numbered areas present conceptions in the order of their development. An exact depiction would also have presented how they dovetail. Shaded areas designate conceptions that arise in the course of correcting earlier ideas.

The Modus Operandi of Theological Science

First, we were all taught that a *hypothesis* is an assumption developed in order to solve a problem. If it proves helpful for that purpose, then it becomes generally accepted and takes on the status of a *theory.*

Second, we were taught that the similarities and differences said to be present in the first three Gospels present a problem—*the Synoptic problem*. Since these similarities extend "right down to wording and sentence structure," there is allegedly a *literary-critical problem*. The literary interrelationships between the Gospels of Matthew, Mark, and Luke are said to demand clarification.

Third, we were taught that the best solution for this problem has turned out to be the *two-source theory*. This theory assumes that Matthew and Luke used Mark as a source, along with another source called the *Logienquelle* (the *sayings source* or simply *Q*), so named because its content consists mainly of sayings. In addition, Matthew and Luke incorporated additional traditions available to them in oral or even written form, and their writings preserve this unique material as depicted in Figure 1.3, part A. We were instructed to pay special attention to similarities as we compared Synoptic texts. Now, despite the similarities, differences in wording of these Gospels inevitably catch the eye; to account for these differences the instructor holds ready a wide selection of individual explanations. These range from the informative ("Here the evangelist has improved the style of his source.") to the improbable ("Here the evangelist has used, along with his source, a special tradition."). The latter explanation never explains what might induce the evangelist to use this strange procedure of hopping back and forth between source and special tradition!

In the end the authority of the science utterly silences questions. In the 1960s teachers maintained that "this two-source theory has proven itself in research to the extent that one is inclined to cease calling it 'theory' (in the sense of 'hypothesis'). One is justified rather in regarding it as an assured result."[15]

But we students were never told that the two-source theory resulted from no thorough investigation of the biblical data, but rather is a transitional phase in the course of a discussion. That discussion paid little attention to its subject matter. In other sciences data are first scrutinized, a problem discovered, and a solution sought. But in this case only a conjecture was put forth regarding

15. Willi Marxsen, *Einleitung in das Neue Testament, eine Einführung in ihre Probleme*, 2d ed. (Gütersloh, 1964), 106.

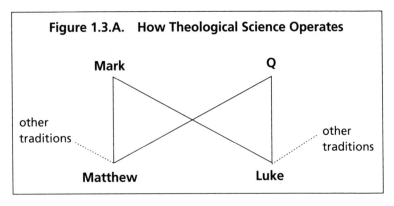

Figure 1.3.A.   How Theological Science Operates

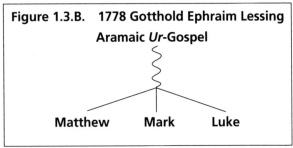

Figure 1.3.B.   1778 Gotthold Ephraim Lessing

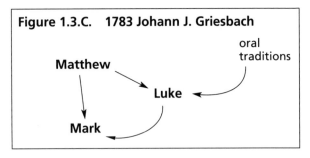

Figure 1.3.C.   1783 Johann J. Griesbach

the origin of the Gospels—not by a theologian or exegetical spe-
cialist but by the philosopher and poet Gotthold Ephraim Lessing
(1729–1781). He made this proposal in an essay written in 1778,
but it was first published posthumously in 1784 as "New Hypotheses concerning the Evangelists regarded as merely human Historians." The title betrays the bias which animated the conjecture.
In addition, Lessing is familiar to us not only as the author of the

play *Nathan the Wise*, which contains the famous ring parable, but also as the editor of the Reimarus fragments.

In a dubious reinterpretation of Eusebius (*Historia ecclesia* 3.24.6) Lessing conjectured that Matthew, Mark, and Luke were mere translations of an original Aramaic gospel of the Nazarenes, "which each one made as best he could" (Fig. 1.3, part B). Corollaries of Lessing's position, as others elaborated on it, are as follows:

1. The original gospel is no longer extant. (Christians are still reproached with this charge by Muslims!)
2. The original gospel—in view of the differences between Matthew, Mark, and Luke—cannot be reconstructed.
3. The extant Gospels furnish imprecise, inept, arbitrary translations of the original. Thus they give no reliable tradition.
4. Inasmuch as they are only the literary remains of the original gospel, they are not to be regarded as independently valid tradition.
5. The relationship between the Gospels is literary. The writers are not eyewitnesses and hearers of that which Jesus said and did.
6. The Synoptic problem is established as a literary-critical problem.

Lessing's conjecture, along with its implications, would soon probably have been forgotten had not the theologians outdone each other in seeking to use this poet's idea. What came to pass was the very thing that God's Word had long since prophesied: "For the time will come when men will not put up with sound doctrine. Instead, to suit their own desires, they will gather around them a great number of teachers to say what their itching ears want to hear. They will turn their ears away from the truth and turn aside to myths" (2 Tim. 4:3–4).

Matthew As a Source Gospel

The first theologian to show great zeal in declaring allegiance to Lessing was Johann J. Griesbach (1745–1812).[16] He has been

---

16. All dates, as well as the citations, in this section are from Theodor Zahn, "§50 Geschichte des 'synoptischen Problems,'" in *Einleitung in das Neue Testament*, vol. 2 (Leipzig, 1899): 182–99.

followed by all subsequent historical-critical theologians in that they all regard the interrelationships of the gospels as a literary-critical problem and do not allow the gospels to speak as independent witnesses, either direct or indirect, to a set of events.

In 1783 Griesbach first promulgated his source-critical theory of how the Gospels made use of each other, "consciously in full agreement with Lessing over what constituted a truly historical outlook and departing from Lessing only with respect to specific results": "The apostle Mt wrote in Greek on the basis of what he himself knew without recourse to older sources. Lc [wrote] his gospel on the basis of his researches into the still fluid tradition and with reference to Mt's gospel; Mc used excerpts from both of these gospels to present his own gospel as a summary" (Fig. 1.3, part C).

What about the traditions from the early church that give information about the origins of the Gospels? Griesbach focused only on those in which he found supporting evidence for his hypothesis. The rest he arbitrarily declared to be "sheer fabrication" and "worthless fables."

How scientific "scientific" theology is becomes obvious as we consider what Griesbach was really saying: Historical church tradition—which possessed incontrovertible validity for friend and foe alike in the second century, when some were still alive who could declare what was bogus—was branded a lie by a "scientist" at the end of the eighteenth century! Yet this view so thoroughly discredited the tradition that its claim to truth no longer was taken seriously by historical-critical theology.

Mark As a Source Gospel

Beginning in 1786 Gottlob Christian Storr (1746–1805) championed another source-critical theory of how the Gospels made use of each other. But his view differed from Griesbach's in that Storr held Mark to be the oldest Gospel, a writing based—just as ancient tradition states—on Peter's reminiscences. Matthew, in spite of his knowledge of the facts, used Mark, as did Luke, who did not know of Matthew (Fig. 1.3, part D).

An A.D. 35 Source Gospel

In 1794 Johann Gottfried Eichhorn (1752–1827) followed Lessing's hypothesis of a (lost) original gospel, without mentioning his indebtedness to Lessing for the idea. He quite surpassed even the poet, however, in concocting a literary fantasy:

He ventured a specific date for the hypothetical original gospel: A.D. 35, never offering reasons for his utter assurance that this was the specific year.

He claimed, without basis, that the missing gospel was written by a student of an apostle, thus robbing the gospel of any eyewitness authority.

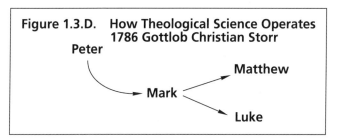

Figure 1.3.D.   How Theological Science Operates
1786 Gottlob Christian Storr

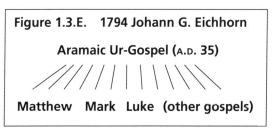

Figure 1.3.E.   1794 Johann G. Eichhorn

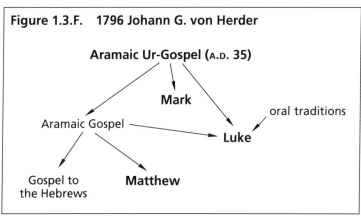

Figure 1.3.F.   1796 Johann G. von Herder

Unlike Lessing, he did not trace the canonical Gospels back to the original. Rather Eichhorn's scenario describes the rise of innumerable gospels between A.D. 35–60; these gospels, in variegated combination, become the sources for both canonical and the extra-canonical gospels (Fig. 1.3, part E).

An Oral Source Gospel

This ongoing formation of hypotheses followed a definite pattern: *one takes up the hypothesis of one's predecessor, partially in agreement and partially in disagreement.* The subject matter of the Gospels did not enter into this discussion. The engine which generates science's "progress" is not investigation of the subject matter but rather criticism of the opinion of one's predecessors on the basis of one's own previously-decided opinion.

In 1796 Johann Gottfried von Herder (1744–1803)—following Storr but disagreeing both with early church tradition and with Griesbach and Eichhorn—declared Mark the oldest extant Gospel. The poet Herder brought honor to himself by inventing a story which builds on Eichhorn's hypothesis: The original gospel, whose compass he sees as does Eichhorn, was formulated orally and transmitted to future missionaries, evangelists, and servants of the Word. For convenience these "students" immediately reduced this information to written form. One of them was Mark; several decades later, probably in Rome, he wrote down his version of these notes "under the supervision of Peter, James, and John in Greek, but accurately." The same original oral gospel, says Herder, gave rise to a complete Aramaic gospel; this gospel lives on, albeit in altered form, in the Greek Gospel penned by Matthew. Luke also used this Aramaic gospel, along with his own notes and eyewitness reports (Fig. 1.3, part F).

When fantasy is given full reign in the matter of Synoptic origins, there are no limits to how far it will wander. Each person lets it run as far as he is able to follow it.

Matthew and Mark as Source Gospels

In 1808 Johann Leonhard Hugh (1765–1846) returned to Matthew as the oldest Gospel; Mark used it and Luke borrowed from both Matthew and Mark (Fig. 1.3, part G).

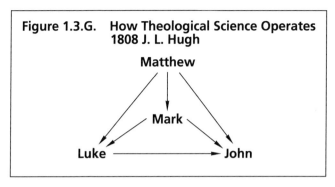

Figure 1.3.G.   How Theological Science Operates
1808 J. L. Hugh

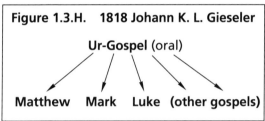

Figure 1.3.H.   1818 Johann K. L. Gieseler

A Fixed Oral Tradition

In 1818 Johann Karl Ludwig Gieseler (1792–1854) became the first to reckon seriously with a somewhat lengthy period of oral transmission. This tradition, maintained Gieseler, gave rise to a fixed form of the Gospel, but this form was itself flexibly conceived. Gieseler took Herder's hypothesis seriously, although Herder, by assuming an immediate written form for the Gospel, contradicted him from the start. The oral gospel, which was first transmitted in Aramaic, then later in Greek, became Gieseler's source for both the canonical and extra-canonical gospels (Fig. 1.3, part H). He did not consider the possibility that a body of eyewitness testimony might have furnished the background. Like all the others he was under the spell of Lessing's "conjecture."

A Collection of Sayings

Friedrich Schleiermacher (1768–1834) first stated his views on the problem in 1817, actually a bit prior to Gieseler. He made no allowance for an oral or written original gospel, nor for a reciprocal use by the various writers of each others' works. Instead he assumed "a great number of small, written fragments of narratives," which "form the connecting link of the Gospels, the foundation and the beginning of the gospel writings in their entirety" (Fig. 1.3, part I).[17]

In 1832, leaning heavily on certain of Papias' words in Eusebius without carefully considering their context, he hit on the idea—which had occurred to no one in the previous centuries of Christian thought—that there must have existed a collection of Jesus-sayings (Fig. 1.3, part J). This so-called sayings-source was, therefore, not discovered through an investigation of the data in the Gospels but through an interpretation of Papias' statement, by no means the only interpretation possible. This is how the second element in the two-source hypothesis was found. That's how scientific science is!

Mark and Luke As Sources

In 1838 Christian G. Wilke (1788–1854) argued once more in favor of Marcan priority (Fig. 1.3, part K). In addition, he assumed that Matthew had used both Mark and Luke—contra Griesbach, who had argued that Luke used Matthew. In this game anything goes; each person proposes just about anything he wishes.

The Two-Source Hypothesis

Christian H. Weiße (1801–1866) in 1838 was actually the first to propound the two-source hypothesis (Fig. 1.3, part L), the possibility of which had opened up with Schleiermacher's reading of Papias. It was some time, however, before this theory found general acceptance; first *Tendenz* criticism made its appearance.

Pauline-Judaistic Source Conflict

That view was first championed by Ferdinand Christian Baur (1792–1860), who rightly deplored the arbitrary give-and-take of Synoptic studies. He championed the view in 1847 that no solution would be found until "the leading ideas, the tendency or bias, of each Gospel are determined." The historian's fantasy puts forth blossoms: The Gospels are not illuminated but assaulted.

17. Ibid., 188.

Figure 1.3.I.   How Theological Science Operates
1817 Friedrich Schleiermacher

Fragments → Matthew, Mark, Luke

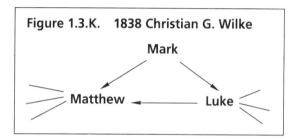

Figure 1.3.J.   1832 Schleiermacher

"Sayings source" = Ur-Matthew

Figure 1.3.K.   1838 Christian G. Wilke

Mark → Matthew ← Luke

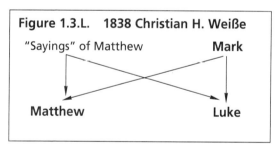

Figure 1.3.L.   1838 Christian H. Weiße

"Sayings" of Matthew   Mark

Matthew   Luke

A Pauline proto-Luke, Baur suggests, lashed out against the Judaistic Matthew. The later version of Luke attempted to mediate between the Pauline and the Judaistic standpoints. Meanwhile, Mark—who used Matthew and either the earlier or the later version of Luke—adopted a neutral position, since he was writing on the far side of the disputes raging during the apostolic era (Fig. 1.3, part M).[18]

18. Ibid., 189.

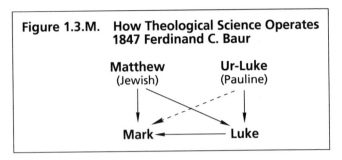

Figure 1.3.M.   How Theological Science Operates
                 1847 Ferdinand C. Baur

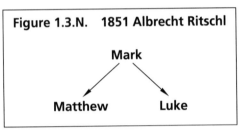

Figure 1.3.N.   1851 Albrecht Ritschl

Figure 1.3.O.   1854 Adolf Hilgenfeld

Hebrew original → Matthew → Mark → Luke

An Original Hebrew Gospel

While Albrecht Ritschl (1822–1889) in 1851 came out in favor of Marcan priority (Fig. 1.3, part N), Adolf Hilgenfeld (1823–1907) in 1854 revived the notion of an original Hebrew gospel from which could be traced a straight line of descent to Matthew, Mark, and Luke (Fig. 1.3, part O).

Two Matthews

Bernhard Weiß (1827–1918) in 1861 proposed a compromise between schools of hypotheses that depended on a (lost) original gospel, on the one hand, and those that worked rather from the basis of source-critical theory, on the other. He sought to mediate between Marcan and Matthean priority and between a critical mentality and fidelity to ancient church tradition. Weiß's solution posited an earlier version of Matthew, one that was first written in

Aramaic and then in Greek. This proto-Matthew served, with orally transmitted stories from Peter, as the source of Mark (Fig. 1.3, part P). This early version of Matthew lacked the first two chapters of the later version and the passion and resurrection narratives. Similarly, Matthew and Luke used the early version of Matthew and Mark—though Luke also possessed an additional source.

An Improved Two-Source Theory

In 1863 Heinrich Julius Holtzmann (1832–1910) finally came up with an improved version of Weiß' two-source theory (Fig. 1.3, part Q). It is said to have gained currency because it satisfied ideological trends of the moment. According to Rainer Riesner, the two-source theory gave contemporary theology what it had been seeking:

> A. Schweitzer remarks in his history of life-of-Jesus research, referring to the two liberal lives-of-Jesus by D. Schenkel and K. H.

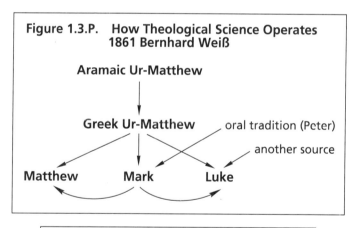

Figure 1.3.P.   How Theological Science Operates
1861 Bernhard Weiß

Aramaic Ur-Matthew

Greek Ur-Matthew   oral tradition (Peter)

another source

Matthew   Mark   Luke

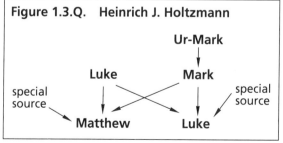

Figure 1.3.Q.   Heinrich J. Holtzmann

Ur-Mark

Luke   Mark

special source   special source

Matthew   Luke

Weizsäcker: "What attracted these writers to the Marcan hypothesis was not so much the authentication which it gave to the detail of Mark, though they were willing enough to accept that, but the way in which this Gospel lent itself to the *a priori* view of the course of the life of Jesus which they unconsciously brought with them. They appealed to Holtzmann because he showed such wonderful skill in extracting from the Marcan narrative the view which commended itself to the spirit of the age as manifested in the [eighteen-] 'sixties.[19]

William R. Farmer goes so far as to argue that "the scientific question regarding the literary relation between our Mark and our Matthew was almost totally overshadowed by a practical necessity: a scientific foundation was needed for the theological quest for the 'historical Jesus.'"[20]

Nevertheless, not until after World War II and the world-wide acceptance of historical-critical theology, did the two-source hypothesis gain general international recognition.

This survey of the history of research is not passed on in all its details merely to inform the reader. It is rather meant to furnish an important insight into so-called *scientific* theology: It is an idle game with contrived possibilities that are set in motion and allowed to bounce off each other like billiard balls. Admittedly, the game is conducted with great seriousness of purpose and expenditure of effort—which can also be said of children's games. *It is a game which gratifies the intellect, which confirms the "I," which tests one's wits and develops talents. And it makes possible a convivial interchange among like-minded colleagues. In short, it is a game which comports perfectly with the tendencies of what the apostle Paul describes as the old man.* That is why some want so much to participate in it. Besides, the person who achieves success wins great personal recognition.

19. Rainer Riesner, "Wie sicher ist die Zwei-Quellen-Theorie?" *Theologische Beiträge* vol. 8.2 (1977): 50. The translation of Albert Schweitzer follows the standard English edition, *The Quest of the Historical Jesus*, trans. by W. Montgomery (London: A. and C. Black, 1948), 203. The German original is *Von Reimarus zu Wrede*, 4th ed. (Tübingen 1926 [=2d ed., 1913]), 203.

20. "A 'Skeleton in the Closet' of Gospel Research," *Biblical Research*, 6 (1961): 40.

Results of Theological Science

What were the consequences of establishing the Synoptic problem, contriving drastically contrasting approaches to its solution, and temporarily resolving it through the two-source theory?

1. Early church tradition, which mediates information to us regarding the origin of the Gospels, was groundlessly discriminated against because tradition got in the way of the modern intellectual games of so-called science.

2. Similarities among Gospels were explained only by purely literary means, while differences were chalked up to redactional activity. Therefore Matthew and Luke, the "secondary witnesses" (as they were now regarded), lost the historical value they were once thought to posses. At best they were merely theologically interesting.

3. Differences between the Marcan *Vorlage* (the version of Mark supposedly used by Matthew and Luke) and its parallels are considerable—not in what was reported so much as in the wording of the reports. So those who embraced the two-source theory were constrained to conclude that Matthew and Luke made very free use of Mark. Only a portion of the differences are explicable; the rest must be attributed to personal theological biases of the Gospel writers.

4. As a result, Mark's Gospel was charged with the same "free use of tradition." Every attempt to derive information about what actually happened from the wording or order of the tradition was therefore discredited as illegitimate historicizing. In the judgment of this "science" the Gospel writers did not pass on what they saw or heard, or what they heard from eyewitnesses and first-hand hearers of the original gospel events. In the eyes of past researchers these writers are merely collectors who use primitive literary means to make arrangements of traditions from various origins. In the eyes of more recent research these writers transmitted theological concepts with which the modern theologian may agree, but which he mostly criticizes.

5. Since Mark, the one Gospel not attributed directly to an eyewitness by the early church, is declared to be the oldest, it is seen as the foundation for the others. This robs Mark of

confirmation from the other Gospels, since they are literarily dependent on Mark. At the same time the genealogies
and birth narratives are pushed aside as later formations.
We should be acutely aware, however, that the entire dating scheme of New Testament science, insofar as it relates
to the Gospels, is strictly a permutation of the two-source
theory. If this theory falls, so do all the dates associated
with it.

6. The assumption of the sayings-source has this consequence:

> Wherever Matthew and Luke obviously draw on Q, but di-
> verge from each other, the question must be posed: Which
> of the two has modified the common Q source, and what
> were the motives? Here one must ponder whether Mat-
> thew's version is better explained as showing the bias typ-
> ical of Matthew, or whether it is rather the case that Luke's
> version evinces a typically Lucan bias.[21]

*This means that every divergence should be explained by the as-
sumption that biases are at work.* But what could be more
questionable than such an assumption? Since the divergences in individual passages range at most from 5 to 80
percent of the words used, and on a rough average about 40
to 50 percent (not counting divergences due to word order
and other differences), the amount of data which ends up
at the mercy of explanations based purely on personal taste
is considerable indeed! And of course the explanations also
diverge from each other. *The assumption of a sayings-source
turns out, therefore, not to be helpful at all, since it is capable of
accounting for hardly more than 50 percent of the data.*

7. The situation is no better with respect to the assumption
that Mark is the main source behind Matthew and Luke.
Spot checks of pericopes I cited as classic examples of how
the two-source theory operates in the years when I taught
historical-critical theology reveal that in these pericopes
the total agreement among the Synoptic Gospels in the
words used lies between about 8 and 50 percent. The average is roughly 22 percent. Here, too, then, the hypothesis is

21. Klaus Haacker, *Neutestamentliche Wissenschaft* (Wuppertal, 1981), 65.

capable of explaining only a portion of the data and is not of great assistance.

For this reason it is no wonder that discussion of the Synoptic problem is today in full swing once more and that the two-source theory by no means still meets uncontested acceptance. Riesner writes:

> Since the mid-1960s there have been many indications that the situation in Synoptic studies is undergoing significant change. . . . The majority of researchers, it is true, are hanging on to the old theory, but it has lost a good deal of its self-evidentness. Especially in English-speaking quarters there is growing dissatisfaction with the usual solutions. Farmer has announced the appearance of a large new study which will advance further arguments for the "Griesbach hypothesis."[27] But similar work is underway elsewhere, e.g. at the Synoptic studies institute of the University of Nimwegen. Virtually every imaginable solution to the Synoptic problem, no matter how marginal its merits, currently finds advocates. Traditions[28] and multiple-source hypotheses[29] have advocates, and so do theories of "Ur-gospels" (lost original gospels) in various forms: an Ur-Matthew,[30] Ur-Mark,[31] Ur-Luke[32] preceding all the Synoptics, or an Ur-Matthew preceding at least Matthew and Mark.[33] Alongside of these theories one may find the most various source-critical hypotheses imaginable.[22]

Riesner counts at least twenty-two of these theories—almost two dozen!

We have no way of knowing what direction research will go from here. In the near future a certain balance will probably be struck. Later, assuming there is time enough remaining to us, research will receive renewed impetus in some other direction. There will be, however, no real solution, nor can there be, because the problem is not a genuine problem. It did not emerge from painstaking observation of the data. The Synoptic problem is a contrivance that has been foisted onto the Synoptic Gospels from the outside. For what reason? To help us understand God's Word better? Absolutely not.

22. *Theologische Beiträge*, vol. 8.2 (1977): 53–54.

The inventor of the Synoptic problem, Lessing leaves us no doubt regarding his motives; he voiced his attitude toward the Christian faith in unmistakable terms.

> It is true that Lessing wanted public opinion to view him as a friend of Christianity; he did not want to suffer being thrown out of his father's house. But he wrote secretly to his friend Moses Mendelssohn (after Lavater had attempted in vain to convert Mendelssohn from Judaism to Christianity): "You are the only one who may and can write and speak freely in this matter. You are thereby infinitely happier than all the other honest persons who can do nothing more to hasten the overthrow of this hateful edifice of nonsense than to hide behind the pretense of furnishing new bases for it."[23]

Lessing's declared intention played a role in the invention of the Synoptic problem. He met success to an extent that he had probably not even dared to dream. *The so-called Synoptic problem comprises about one-half of the ground on which the imposing edifice of New Testament science has been erected.*

Consequences

That edifice of theological science is thoroughly imbued with the spirit of Lessing, who wrote:

> The measure of man's worth does not lie in the truth which someone possesses, or thinks he possesses, but rather in the sincere effort which he has expended to discover the truth. For it is not the possession, but the investigation of the truth which enlarges those powers in which alone his constantly growing perfection consists. Possession causes one to relax, to become indolent and proud! If God held all truth in his clenched right hand, and in his left the unique, ever lively quest for truth—along with the provision that I would constantly and eternally go astray if I chose the left—and then were to say to me: Choose!, I would humbly opt for the left and say, Father, let this be my lot! The pure truth is for you alone.[24]

23. Günther Dürr, "J. M. Goeze—ein Kämpfer für die Wahrheit der Heiligen Schrift," *Bibel und Gemeinde*, vol. 71: 217.

24. Ibid., 216.

We should, therefore, spare ourselves the illusions of assuming that New Testament science would be seriously shaken through the destruction of one of its bases. The discipline would only become all the more busy, having so much the more work for doctoral and post-doctoral candidates, who would leap into action to draw up new hypotheses to stabilize the edifice. For them a major failure in the discipline's accepted views would turn out to be a stroke of good fortune rather than a disaster.

We are faced with the question, however, of whether we are finally ready to grasp what Lessing actually—though ostensibly humbly—stated before God, that he wished to dispense with the truth. His move was nothing less than a repudiation of the gift of the Father, his unique Son, who is the way, the truth, and the life! Do we wish to follow Lessing any longer?

We would do better to harken to J. M. Goeze, the doughty defender of the most holy faith, who immediately saw through Lessing's pseudo-humility. On the basis of God's Word he could reply to Lessing:

> What does Jesus say to that? "This is eternal life, that they know you, the only true God, and Jesus Christ whom you have sent" (John 3:17). Lessing plainly contradicts this famous dictum of Jesus; now, who deserves our trust? Jesus or Lessing?
>
> Paul states: God desires that all persons be saved and come to the knowledge of the truth [1 Tim. 2:4]. No, says Lessing: the possession of the truth causes one to relax, to become indolent and proud! How much wiser is Lessing here than Paul. Be content, you people, with the same circumstances that Tantalus had to endure. . . .
>
> According to this teaching all the confidence of faith, all gladness in God, all hope of eternal life and even the blessedness of eternal life—all these are foolishness and fantasy. According to this teaching it was idle self-glorification when Paul said: "I know whom I have believed" [1 Tim 1:12]. But that is the nature of this new wisdom through which the alleged friends of Christianity and avowed enemies of Holy Scripture wish to enlighten the world.[25]

25. Ibid.

We must decide: *Either we follow our Lord Jesus in our theological work and cling loyally to his Word, or we pursue theology in the train of poets and philosophers who are declared enemies of our Lord Jesus.*

It is true that if we turn aside from a theology initiated by poets and philosophers we will no longer be regarded as scientists, no matter how thorough and erudite the work we produce. Derision and insult are sure to be our lot, though perhaps not in the same measure that pastor Goeze had to endure.[26] But so what, if afterward our Lord Jesus will say to us: "Well done, thou good and faithful servant?"

Those who feel, however, that they just cannot dispense with science should be reminded once more of what God's Word decreed regarding just this science, long before the birth of Gotthold Ephraim Lessing, who preferred the search for truth—along with eternally going astray—over the truth itself. Such people [of the last days] "are loaded down with sins and are swayed by all kinds of evil desires, always learning but never able to acknowledge the truth. Just as Jannes and Jambres opposed Moses, so also these men oppose the truth—men of depraved minds, who, as far as the faith is concerned, are rejected. But they will not get very far because, as in the case of those men, their folly will be clear to everyone" (2 Tim. 3:6–9).

God has not only foreseen and foretold, however, that which has gone on, and still goes on in Old and New Testament science; it is also fully under his control. We read in his Word that "God sends them a powerful delusion so that they will believe the lie and so that all will be condemned who have not believed the truth but have delighted in wickedness" (2 Thess. 2:11–12).

It is still a time of grace; it is still possible to turn from the perversity that, as we have seen, has too often plagued theology. However: "Today, if you hear his voice, do not harden your hearts. . . ." (Ps. 95:7b–8a), lest you be overwhelmed by the power of delusion God has sent, to your eternal undoing.

26. [Johann Melchior Goeze, a Hamburg pastor, responded in writing to Lessing as Lessing published the Reimarus fragments. Lessing had attended and enjoyed Goeze's sermons. After this he attacked Goeze bitterly. Goeze wrote Lessing a pastorly, carefully worded letter in which he shared Christ with him in the hope he might be converted.]

2

New Testament Criticism in Academic Studies

For anyone who still feels obligated to view historical-critical theology as scientific theology, I would like to demonstrate once more what I showed in chapter 1, this time in the area of academic pedagogy.

Every university theology or divinity (ministerial) student in Germany must take a preliminary New Testament seminar, in which he or she is familiarized with the methodological tools of historical-critical theology in New Testament exegesis. The effects of this seminar are deepened by books that promise to introduce the student to the New Testament, to New Testament exegesis, or to methods of New Testament study. In this seminar the student is, as a rule, confronted with the so-called Synoptic problem and its presumed solution, among other topics. The Synoptic problem is an essential element in assigned readings. For this reason it will be worthwhile to test these readings to determine how the student is introduced to the Synoptic problem and how the theory of Marcan priority is made plausible. This will enable us to test the claims to scientific validity made by historical-critical theology.

First we will analyze a section pertaining to our subject as a whole from an introductory textbook; second, we will go on to a selection of readings from other introductory manuals. To give

an analytical illustration of these procedures I have selected
Georg Strecker and Udo Schnelle, *Einführung in die neutestamentliche Exegese* (*Introduction to New Testament Exegesis*), a book
used in many German universities to acquaint students with the
practice of New Testament exegesis.[1] In some universities where
this book is not the foundational introduction, it is nonetheless
assigned as recommended reading. This handbook stands out as
superior, in many respects, to most other introductory literature.
I concern myself below with pages 46–54 (sections 5.1–5.4.1) of
this book.

An Introductory Approach to the Synoptics

With respect to the eleven titles on Synoptic criticism that
Strecker and Schnelle cite, it is to their credit that they list two op-
ponents of the two-source theory: William R. Farmer's *The Synoptic
Problem: A Critical Analysis*[2] and Hans-Herbert Stoldt, *History and
Criticism of the Marcan Hypothesis*.[3] By mentioning Robert Morgenthaler, *Statistik des neutestamentlichen Wortschatzes*[4] they also
call attention to the statistical investigation of the Synoptics. This
honest concern for objectivity deserves to be acknowledged.

In section 5.1, the impression of objectivity is confirmed
when Strecker defines the Synoptic problem as "the question
whether and how the gospels of Matthew, Mark, and Luke are literarily dependent on each other." "Whether and how"—that
means the literary dependence apparently is not presupposed at
the outset. The appearance, however, is deceptive, for it becomes
clear that the authors define the concept of literary dependence
more narrowly than is normally the case. They extend the concept's validity only to the theory of mutual interdependence.[5]
This means Strecker and Schnelle do not consider the possibility
that the three Synoptic Gospels arose independently from each
other. In section 5.2, accordingly, one encounters this learning

1. Georg Strecker and Udo Schnelle, *Einführung in die neutestamentliche Exegese*, 2d ed. (Göttingen, 1985). Translation of German works quoted in this
chapter are by Robert Yarbrough. Emphasis in each case is the original author's.
2. New York: Macmillan, 1964; repr. ed., Dillsboro, N.C.: Western North
Carolina Press, 1976.
3. Macon, Ga.: Mercer University Press, 1980.
4. Zurich-Frankfurt: Gotthelf, 1958.
5. Strecker and Schnelle, *Einführung*, 48.

objective: "The student should be equipped to make an independent assessment of the literary dependence that exists among the first three Gospels."

The literary dependence is presupposed. Is "an independent assessment" possible within the confines of such a presupposition?

In section 5.3, in the subsection "On the history of the Synoptic problem," the authors manipulate the students' outlook by asserting, "As long as readers regarded the authors of the Gospels as eye-witnesses of the life of Jesus and uncritically . . . accepted early church tradition, the differences among the Gospels posed a problem for only a few." In other words, to maintain that the authors of the Gospels were eyewitnesses appears as a long-abandoned option. Agreement with early church tradition is condemned as "uncritical" at the outset. What student in seminar discussion is going to risk being labeled as uncritical and hopelessly behind the times by raising the possibility that the three Gospels are equally original, in keeping with their own claims and early church tradition? First we read, "The differences among the gospels posed a problem for only a few"; but these few immediately shrink to only one: Augustine.

The authors assert, "Actual research of the Synoptic problem does not begin until the second half of the 18th century, where four hypotheses merit special mention." The hypotheses that arose in the second half of the 18th century are elevated to "actual research of the Synoptic problem." In effect an equation is set out here:

Research=Establishment of Hypotheses

But this is a far cry from the normal concept of science, which would be formulated:

Research=Testing of Hypotheses

In the natural sciences one expects proposed hypotheses to be subjected to empirical testing. In the humanities one should at least expect that proposed hypotheses be confronted with the result of comprehensive investigation.

We have already seen that the history of New Testament criticism offers a hopeless tangle of hypotheses regarding the literary dependence of the Synoptic Gospels, yet the "science" of New Testament introduction reduces the tangle to just four groups—the Ur-Gospel hypothesis, the narrative hypothesis, the tradition hypothesis, and the literary dependence hypothesis—thereby rationalizing and disguising its great abstrusities.

1. The Ur-Gospel Hypothesis

The foundation of this proposal is the thought that "Thus Lessing suspected. . . ." The language is revealing: There were nothing more than thoughts and suspicions to offer. The book states that Johann Gottfried Eichhorn furnished a "comprehensive basis," but one learns nothing of what this basis comprises. The student is simply told that Eichhorn "accepted an Aramaic Ur-Gospel, which lay before each Gospel writer in an altered form." Along with this the Synoptic writers "used additional sources as well." So the student is dished up an adventurous sequence of hypotheses: An Ur-Gospel arises, and it then is reworked into three divergent recensions.

Why? To what purpose? By whom? When? Where? No answer to these questions is given. Instead, the student is supposed to swallow the view that these recensions were mixed together by the Synoptics with additional sources, whose origins lie in equally inscrutable darkness. This is all set before the student as a hypothesis to be taken seriously and from which to deduce that the Gospels presuppose a lengthy literary process. What precision mathematics, that draw positive results from the sum of calculating errors! The only hint that a problem exists comes in the statement that the difficulties behind the Gospels retreat "into the darkness of a lost literature."

2. The Narrative Hypothesis

The narrative hypothesis is not tested against the entirety of the Synoptic data. Its significance is limited by the statement that it has been advanced only in connection with Luke's Gospel. Whether the hypothesis squares with the material contained in Luke is not taken up. The refutation of this hypothesis is not even put into words; it is merely assessed like a teacher sometimes marks a paper, grading it based on the result he or she tacitly expects. The hypothesis is given high marks: "Positively, this hypothesis sees the rise of the Gospels in terms of a process of collecting discrete components into a larger whole." Why this should be thought positive, the student is not told. The verdict must be accepted by faith.

3. The Tradition Hypothesis

Neither is the tradition hypothesis critically examined. It is merely stated. The student is again handed a positive verdict that is set forth like an *ex cathedra* pronouncement: "This thesis is the first to recognize the extensive involvement of oral tradition in the formation of the Gospels."

It is worth pointing out that, just because a hypothesis is re-named a thesis—which is just what takes place in the hypothesis stated above—does not mean that the hypothesis thereby becomes a source of knowledge assured by science. Hypotheses are assumptions, suppositions that things relate in a certain way. They do not in themselves deliver the assured result that things *do* relate that way. One should learn, in the science of New Testament introduction as in mathematics, to distinguish between assertion, presupposition, and proof. A hypothesis is an assertion to be proven, not the proof.

Therefore, the tradition hypothesis does not *prove* "the extensive involvement of oral tradition in the formation of the Gospels"; it merely *presupposes* it. The oral tradition is an assumption that presupposes another assumption: Oral tradition was integral to the formation of the Gospels. The use of a hypothesis at the primary level to establish another hypothesis at a secondary level does not change the primary hypothesis into fact.

What is Strecker and Schnelle's starting point as they weigh the above hypotheses? Are there perhaps specially designated research results behind their assessments? Absolutely not. One starting point is the two-source hypothesis, which is said to be superior to the earlier mentioned hypotheses. Ultimately, however, the starting point is form criticism, which is based on the two-source theory. Form criticism and the two-source hypothesis mutually stabilize and give credence to each other.

4. The Literary Dependence Hypothesis

The literary dependence hypothesis here means that a writer used the writing of another as a source. The literary dependence that this hypothesis posits is not defined by Strecker and

Schnelle. There is no inquiry into what type of literary dependence might be at work, although that concept can refer to any among a wide spectrum of possibilities.[6] Accordingly, there is no possibility of comparing the data in the Gospels with the results that are expected from the type of literary dependence assumed. So the question remains open as to which presuppositions will be capable of validating the literary dependence.

The question of whether we should assume Matthean or Marcan priority is not raised. It is merely answered with distorted information for the unwitting student: "The philologist Karl Lachmann achieved a decisive step toward establishing the literary-dependence hypothesis . . . with the assumption that Mark formed the foundation for Matthew and Luke." It is remarkable how recklessly Strecker and Schnelle pass on this false information. They should have known the truth, had they actually read Stoldt's *History and Criticism of the Marcan Hypothesis*, which they list in their selection of recommended studies.

What Lachmann actually said was this:

> If it is *obvious* that they (Matthew and Luke)—in spite of this extremely high degree of agreement—nevertheless *did not have a copy of Mark which they imitated, as a basis*, what other assumption, indeed, is left, than that *this Akoluthia, followed by all (three) as if it had been prescribed to them, had already been authoritatively and definitively determined by the evangelical tradition before their own literary activity?*

Stoldt rightly concludes from this statement by Lachmann that *"Lachmann clearly rules out the contention that Matthew and Luke used the Gospel of Mark; rather he assumes a preevangelical order of the narrative sequence determined authoritatively by tradition."*[7]

Strecker and Schnelle next tell the student that Christian Gottlob Wilke and Christian Hermann Weiße proved, indepen-

---

6. See chapter 8.
7. Stoldt, *History and Criticism*, 148. The Latin for the first paragraph runs:
   Si in hoc summo consensu tamen illos Marci exemplum quod imitarentur propositum non habuisse manifestum est, quid quam ipse scriberent, auctoritate ac traditione quadam evangelica constitutum et conprimatum fuisse dicamus?

dently of each other, that Mark is the common source for Matthew and Luke. Although earlier there was sufficient space for the hypotheses that were rejected, now the student finds not one argument to illustrate how Wilke and Weiße arrived at their findings. The student must take it on blind trust that the required proofs for the two-source hypothesis have been set forth in these books, to which it would be quite difficult to gain access. But so that we may be better informed, let us weigh Stoldt's analysis of Wilke and Weiße.

With respect to Wilke, Stoldt writes:

> 1) In his arguments Wilke presupposed that which he had yet to prove ("since Mark is always the one accompanied"). He always based the substance of his comparative synoptic columns on Mark. He could sustain his allegation that the Gospel of Mark formed the basic text and source of Matthew and Luke only by repeatedly resorting to a *petitio principii*.
> 2) His changes in the text (interpolations and eliminations) are arbitrary and not objectively justified since they are not textually documented and cannot be demonstrated in a single case. Already, they contain *in nuce* the assumption of a proto-Mark, functioning as an auxiliary hypothesis.
> 3) Wilke did not succeed in proving his thesis of Matthew's dependence on Luke. Wilke neither investigated nor answered the unavoidable question of where Luke obtained the narrative material that he holds in common with Matthew (see Wilke's preface).[8]

Regarding Weiße's argumentation, Stoldt comments:

> Both of Weisse's attempts to explain the *origin* of the common extra-Marcan material in Matthew and Luke within the framework of the Marcan hypothesis must be considered failures. The logia source has proved itself incapable of accommodating elements that do not consist of dominical sayings. The "lost" earlier form of the canonical Mark, the proto-Mark which Weisse had constructed in order to explain those elements, has proved to be nonexistent, and attempts to document it have long since been abandoned. . . .
> In addition to this exaggeration of expression, Weisse's scholarly mentality was characterized by a certain unscrupulousness in

8. Ibid., 44.

demonstrating proofs. One example of this was his inadmissible appropriation of the deceased Schleiermacher for the purpose of substantiating his own point of view about Luke's usage of the logia source. Another was the frivolity with which Weisse transferred pericopes from the sayings collection to the proto-Mark, even including parts which had never before been placed there.

Moreover, Weisse was not skilled at sustaining an argument. He constantly found himself in difficulties with his hypothesis, but he tried to surmount his difficulties by employing a pseudo-argumentation which, as a rule, was so transparent as to expose its vulnerability. . . . Because of this Weisse repeatedly felt inclined to ask in advance for the indulgence of the reader, and to implore understanding of the decisions he had to make in regard to the hypothesis—even if these decisions were contrary to the facts. . . .

All this . . . makes it clear that, in reality, Weisse constantly found himself and his hypothesis on the verge of calamity. In this connection it is worth noting that almost every time he himself recognized the immediate difficulty confronting his hypothesis. He saw it clearly—and drew not a single conclusion from it! On the contrary, he tried again and again to get over the particular difficulty either by some very daring action, or at worst by glossing it over. In this manner, slowly but surely, his entire argumentation grew into a system of makeshifts. Would it not have been better for Weisse to draw a different conclusion from his difficulties—i.e., to reevaluate thoroughly the whole basis of his two-source theory?[9]

If what Stoldt reports is true,[10] can one still speak of Wilke and Weiße having *proven* the two-source hypothesis? Even if Strecker and Schnelle do not agree with Stoldt, should not they at least have mentioned him in this connection? Or was listing the title of Stoldt's work among the relevant literature just a ruse?

In section 5.4.2 Strecker and Schnelle state, "The order of pericopes found in the Synoptics is a convincing argument for Marcan priority." But their discussion amounts to nothing more than question-begging; the very point to be proven is continually presupposed, that Matthew and Luke used Mark. The authors flatly assert: "After 14:1 Matthew clearly follows Mark's or-

9. Ibid., 65–67.
10. Stoldt's assessment of Weiße is substantially corroborated by Farmer, *Synoptic Problem*, 22–25.

dering of pericopes, wherever he makes use of Marcan material."
This reference to the rearrangement of pericopes only works *if*
the Marcan arrangement is presupposed. What speaks *against*
this assertion—the quite different construction in Matthew 8–
9—is presented as evidence *for* the assertion. The conclusion one
might expect—that Matthew did *not* use Mark—is not drawn
from the fact that in Matthew 8–9 five pericopes do *not* follow
Mark's order. It is rather asserted that here Matthew preferred a
different order due to the peculiar nature of the work he wished
to compose. With this the process of circular reasoning is complete: Whether Matthew follows Mark's order, or whether he
does not, he is still dependent on Mark.

Strecker and Schnelle, as if they sat next to Matthew at his
desk as he wrote, risk the adventuresome statement, "Matthew
combines the calling (Mk 3:13–19) and sending out (Mk 6:7–11)
of the disciples, adding to these accounts selected individual
words of Jesus, to make one large commissioning sermon. In addition he makes use of isolated rearrangements of individual dominical sayings." This pictures an autonomous author who arbitrarily weaves material together that he sets before his readers as
a discourse from Jesus' lips. Would a disciple of Jesus handle the
words of his Lord and Master in this fashion? This rather would
seem to reflect Strecker and Schnelle's own mind. The mode of
thinking of twentieth-century theologians is imposed on the
New Testament.

In sum, the order of pericopes is said to argue in favor of Marcan priority. But in that case, every divergence in order speaks
against Matthew having used Mark. Strecker and Schnelle trans-
form such divergences into alterations of the Marcan original. In
this fashion, they steadily presuppose that which they first need
to prove—that Matthew used the Gospel of Mark.

With respect to Luke's Gospel the same process takes place:
"Luke undertakes . . . rearrangement of pericopes. . . . replaces . . .
reworks . . . unfolds . . . changed the order . . .". All of these ac-
tivities, spoken of Luke as if they were facts being reported, could
only have been accomplished by Luke if he had used Mark's Gospel as a source. But that is precisely the question! It is not even
answered through the agreement in order of pericopes. Rather it
is less effectively answered by explanatory helps intended to
overcome the difficulties posed by divergences in the order of

pericopes. According to Strecker and Schnelle's own list, Luke lacks thirty-two pericopes found in Mark, a decisive objection to the assumption that Mark's Gospel lay before Luke and was used by him. But Strecker and Schnelle take no notice of this; in fact, they even use the Marcan pericopes missing from Luke to explain "Luke's outline, which diverges sharply from that of Mark." So one unknown quantity is used to explain another; the authors summarize by stating that "based on the order of pericopes, Mark's Gospel is the common center for the Gospels of Matthew and Luke."

"A further indication of Marcan priority," continue Strecker and Schnelle, are "improvements in language and content that Matthew and Luke carry out on the Marcan text." Once again this is circular reasoning; something is viewed as an indication of Marcan priority that already assumes Marcan priority. Only if Mark's text lay before Matthew and Luke and was used by them as a source could they have carried out improvements in language and content. But whether they did this requires proof. Perhaps it is true that Matthew's and Luke's language works on a higher level; perhaps their presentation at some points appears to improve on Mark's content. Still, discernible differences between Mark, on the one hand, and the formulation of Matthew or Luke, on the other, fall far short of indicating Marcan priority. A difference does not necessarily point to an alteration. Improved content does not necessarily point to direct augmentation of what Mark wrote. Variegated formulations of the same subject matter can arise independently of each other. These "alterations to the Marcan text in language and content" beg the question; they do not themselves indicate Marcan priority.

Undeterred, the authors write as if passing along established facts, "Matthew smooths [whatever that actually means] . . . inserts the words he prefers . . . carries out changes in vocabulary. . . . Luke makes changes . . . uses foreign words only in translation or even rejects them totally . . . replaces simple verbs with composite verbs [verbs formed by prefixing one or more prepositions] . . . replaces the paratactic *kai* with *de* . . . ". Without even the shadow of a proof appearing on the horizon, third-level hypotheses are palmed off as facts on the student, who is in no position to make an independent judgment.

At certain points one finds outright distortions in Strecker and Schnelle: "Mt 16:24 avoids the repetition of *akolouthein*." But so does Mark, according to the reading attested in the better manuscripts. As an example of "replacing simple verbs with composite verbs" Luke 8:28 is cited, where *anakrazein* is used instead of *krazein*. A classical philologist might raise the question of whether Luke's usage is stylistically better, or whether the difference is simply the result of the contrasting context in which the sentence appears. But let us leave that to the side; I content myself with some statistical data on the use of composite verbs in the Synoptics:

Anakrazein (a composite verb) appears in Mark two times, Luke three times; it does not appear in Matthew.

Krazein (not a composite verb) appears in Matthew twelve times, Mark ten times, and Luke three times.

Composite verbs occur in Matthew 243 times, Mark 239 times, and Luke 418 times.[11] If composite verbs indicate higher style, Mark is more elevated than Matthew, since composite verbs occur with relatively greater frequency in Mark.

If we consider composite verbs preceded by two prepositions, Matthew has twelve occurrences, Mark fourteen, and Luke thirty-one. Some of these appear more than once; Matthew uses a total of eight different composite verbs preceded by two prepositions, Mark, ten, and Luke, twenty. In both cases, if composite verbs indicate higher style, Mark's style is more elevated than is Matthew's.[12]

State Strecker and Schnelle: "A further argument for Marcan priority is the quantity of material. Only three pericopes . . . and a few sayings [found in Mark] . . . appear in neither Matthew nor Luke." Once again Stoldt's study, which they cite in their list of important works, is not consulted. There one finds, not only the "three pericopes" and "a few sayings" cited by Strecker and Schnelle, but also some 180 "minor additional details in Mark

11. According to Morgenthaler, *Statistik*.
12. Ibid., 160, 162.

that extend beyond the text of Matthew and Luke, including passages where either Matthew or Luke are lacking."[13]

Strecker and Schnelle continue: "Word statistics also speak in favor of Marcan priority. For of the 11,078 words in Mark, one finds in shared sections of Matthew 8555 words and of Luke 6737 words." But that is rather evidence for the opposite conclusion: Of the words used by Mark, which Matthew and Luke allegedly used as a source, only 77.22 percent are found in Matthew and just 60.81 percent in Luke.

Strecker and Schnelle do see the need to hold a modified version of the usual two-source hypothesis, because otherwise they cannot explain Luke's omission of Mark 6:45–8:26: "All we can be sure of is the assumption that 6:45–8:26 did not yet appear, or perhaps was no longer contained, in the copy of Mark that lay before Luke." What is the justification for this assumption? That it is needed? Do we wish to continue to try to cover debts with more debts instead of finally admitting the bankruptcy of the two-source hypothesis?

What Strecker and Schnelle have done plugs one hole by tearing open another. Historical criticism sees Matthew and Luke as being written at about the same time. The assumption is that Matthew had access to a complete copy of Mark, while Luke used a copy that was incomplete or defective. But questions immediately arise:

If it was incomplete, why does no trace of a copy of the original version remain?

Within the ten or fifteen years that historical criticism posits between the writing of Mark and Matthew, how does one account for an incomplete Gospel of Mark being expanded by means of pericopes varying in content?

Who carried out this expansion?

How could it have taken place and been spread so rapidly that it came into Matthew's hands?

How could the defects in Luke's copy of Mark have arisen, since the text must not have been defective at the beginning or at the end, but in the middle? And how did defects

13. Stoldt, *History and Criticism*, 11–18.

arise in such a way that the pericopes preceding and following the omitted portion were preserved intact?

Is there any analogy for this in the tradition history of ancient manuscripts?

Such questions, which rapidly expose the untenability of the
hypothesis, are never raised. Instead, one unknown quantity is
adduced to explain another, and the student is hoodwinked.

There are still other reasons why Strecker and Schnelle regard the two-source hypothesis in its classical form as needing
modification: material exists that is unique to Mark, and minor additional details found in Matthew and Luke extend beyond Mark. Strecker and Schnelle regard the two-source hypothesis in its classical form as needing modification, partly
due to the existence of material that is unique to Mark, and
also due to the minor agreements between Matthew and Luke
against Mark.[14] But the hypothesis needs only be augmented,
they say, by adding the assumption that Matthew and Luke
did not have access to the canonical Mark, but rather to a reworked recension, Deutero-Mark, which was characterized by
"smoothing" [Glättungen].

While "smoothing" still is not defined, in view of the examples already cited, it would have to include omissions and additions made for unknown reasons, changes in verb tense and conjunctions, switching of prepositions, and rearrangements of
verses, both in part and in toto. In short, every kind of difference
between Mark on the one hand and Matthew and Luke on the
other must be interpreted as "smoothing." The poor reader never
learns just how Matthew and Luke are "smoother" than Mark—
and it should be added that the concept of "smoothing" is not
standard usage in either the literary sciences or classical philol-
ogy. Certainly the history of Mark's composition is artificially
complicated by the invention of a Deutero-Mark. It demands:

1. The rise of Proto-Mark, which is identical with modern
   Mark;
2. Smoothing of Proto-Mark to become Deutero-Mark;

14. Ibid., 18ff.

3. The rise of a defective Deutero-Mark (This presupposes a longer tradition history and a broad geographical distribution for Deutero-Mark, since otherwise the defectiveness would have been discovered immediately.);
4. The rise of Matthew, using the nondefective Deutero-Mark;
5. The rise of Luke, using the defective Deutero-Mark;
6. Total destruction of the defective Deutero-Mark used by Luke;
7. Total destruction, of the Deutero-Mark used by Matthew, and of all other copies of the nondefective Deutero-Mark, so that not one trace of the recension remained in the textual tradition, and
8. Exclusive transmission of the unsmoothed Proto-Mark, although since its rise it had been superseded by the smoothed Deutero-Mark.

The authors prefer, probably wisely, to maintain discreet silence on the question of how long this absolutely improbable drama took to unfold.

All the arguments that have long been advanced against the hypothesis of an Ur-Mark are just as decisive in refuting an alleged Deutero-Mark. This *deus ex machina* is in no position to solve the problems of the two-source hypothesis.

The above must suffice for an examination of Strecker and Schnelle. Now we turn to other introductory manuals designed for students to see if a selection of characteristic statements bears out the same disturbing tendencies.

Other Introductory Approaches

Marxsen

Willi Marxsen, *Einleitung in das Neue Testament, eine Einführung in ihre Probleme*,[15] bases Marcan priority solely on Lachmann's observation:

C. Lachmann (ThStKr 1835) made the decisive and really pioneering observation in the context of hypotheses of literary borrowing when he determined: Mt and Lk agree only at those points where they agree with Mk; but when they add material not found in Mk,

15. (4th ed., Gütersloh 1978), 119–26. Citations below are from 122, 125.

they insert it at various places—this can only be explained by assuming that Mk furnished the outline for the additions made by both Mt and Lk.

This short excerpt misleads the reader in a number of ways. First, the reader is led to think that the entire sentence from before the dash (—) is a direct or at least indirect quote from Lachmann. In fact, only the first half can be traced, to some extent, back to Lachmann. He never wrote anything resembling the second half but rather stated just the opposite. According to Lachmann, Matthew and Luke did not insert material into the Marcan framework; he stated that Matthew's original sayings collection was later stuffed full of narratives by others.[16]

Second, this latter half of the sentence that contradicts Lachmann is not a factual observation but rather a mere supposition that is laid down as fact: "Matthew and Luke used Mark." But that is precisely what Lachmann could not accept.[17] Material not found in Mark could have been "inserted at various places" by Matthew and Luke only if the text of Mark lay before them and therefore provided the same context for their particular material. What is adduced as an observation made by Lachmann is neither from Lachmann, nor an observation, but simply an unsubstantiated assertion.

Third, Marxsen's "explanation," which is set forth as an apparent observation, explains nothing; it merely expresses an assumption that has been credited falsely to Lachmann. Marxsen tells us that "this observation . . . leads to the two-source theory as it is accepted today." If indeed it does, this underscores the questionable origin of the theory. What true theory must be justified by using falsehood and hidden hypothetical presuppositions? Marxsen draws three wide-ranging conclusions from the two-source theory:

"One can now state that Matthew and Luke, at least, could hardly have been direct witnesses of the Jesus event. Their dependence on literary sources speaks against it. . . ." In this first conclusion, literary dependence, which Marxsen never proves but rather simply asserts, is taken up to call into question the his-

16. Stoldt, *History and Criticism*, 48.
17. Ibid., 148, 44.

torical reliability of Matthew and Luke in their testimony to the Jesus event. If not the major intention of the two-source theory, that is at least the result.

"Accordingly, it is to be observed that Mark by no means possessed 'canonical' validity to Matthew and Luke. They rather handle their source 'critically' and alter the text passed along to them with great freedom." For the second conclusion something again is reported as fact which is merely a questionable inference from an untested hypothesis. Since historical-critical theology commonly supposes that one has proceeded scientifically just by giving birth to a hypothesis and then arguing in its favor, Marxsen sees no reason to test his hypothesis against the full range of relevant data.

The third conclusion proceeds: "Since, however, this independent handling of the sources by the writers of the longer gospels [Matthew and Luke] is not sheer caprice, but obviously is part of their conception, the two-source theory offers decisive assistance for exegesis: for the distinctive outlook of each respective writer of the longer gospels comes to expression precisely in how they vary from their sources."

Here the chain of dependent hypotheses is complete:

1. Matthew and Luke are literarily dependent on Mark.
2. That dependence is not shown in the data; nevertheless, Marxsen is not willing to give up the hypothesis, but instead (probably without being aware of it) inserts another next to it: Matthew and Luke handle Mark critically.
3. In order not to make this critical handling appear to be "sheer caprice," a "conception" of "the writers of the larger Gospels" is supposed.
4. The interpretation of "the writers of the larger Gospels" is carried out by noting their divergences from the Marcan original.

In other words, the entire handling of the three synoptists is based on an untested hypothesis, which was established with the help of an untruth.

Conzelmann and Lindemann

A standard student handbook of New Testament study, *Arbeitsbuch zum Neuen Testament* by H. Conzelmann and A. Lindemann, invites the reader, "Let us now test the tenability of our preliminary hypothesis—that Mark was the (or a) source used by Matthew—by examining some individual pericopes."[18]

In most literature of this sort it is unusual for the insight to be stated that the proposed hypothesis requires testing. But how does the testing proceed? The data in their entirety are not tested; two individual pericopes are plucked out for examination: Mark 2:1–12 and Mark 4:30–32.

Now the parable of the mustard seed (Mark 4:30–32), since it is directly quoting the teaching of Jesus, is something of a special case; one would *a priori* expect greater agreement in parallel passages. We will come back to that below. But even in the pericope of the paralytic the occurrence of dominical (Jesus' own) words is unusually high. In Figure 2.1, using sections of Mark 2:1–12 for a base of comparison we see the difference in the percentage of

Figure 2.1

The Healing of the Paralytic:
A Comparison of Identical Words among the Gospels

	Mark/Matt./ Luke	Mark/Matt.	Mark/Luke
2:1–4 (59 words):	2 *iw*	3 *iw*	10 *iw*
2:5–7 (42 words):	8 *iw*	20 *iw*	17 *iw*
2:12 (22 words):	4 *iw*	4 *iw*	6 *iw*
Total (123 words):	**14 *iw* (11.38%)**	**27 *iw* (21.95%)**	**23 *iw* (18.70%)**

Of the seventy-three total words in the Greek text of Mark 2:8–11, sixty-two (84.93 percent) directly quote Jesus. The percentage of agreement becomes:

2:8–11 (73 words)	38 *iw* (52.05%)	47 *iw* (64.38%)	43 *iw* (58.90%)

Therefore, the number of identical words is markedly higher (though by no means total) when Jesus' words are recorded.

18. H. Conzelmann and A. Lindemann, *Arbeitsbuch zum Neuen Testament*, 5th ed. (Tübingen, 1980), 54–61. The citations below are from 56–58.

identical words in passages that include few or no dominical words with the percentage in passages consisting mainly of dominical words. The abbreviation *iw* stands for the number of identical words:[19]

Conzelmann and Lindemann state that ". . . along with such differences, however, there are also extensive agreements . . . so that a complete literary independence may be regarded as improbable. The key question is: Which version is more likely to be derivable from the other?" Here an all too facile equation is set up: In spite of considerable differences, the extensive agreements still provide proof for literary dependence. No thought is given to alternative explanations of how such agreement might have come into being. I have already mentioned one possibility—the writers' efforts to pass on Jesus' words as precisely as possible. Similarities might also arise because identical content limits the variety of words available to a faithful recorder.

Conzelmann and Lindemann, however, do not answer the question of how great the amount of similarities must be to indicate literary dependence in cases where identical content is passed on. Everything remains subjective and free-floating, although scientific rigor is claimed for their results. Using such an approach, their preliminary hypothesis is not tested. Since no falsification is permitted, no verification is possible. That which needs to be proven is presupposed—literary dependence. The discussion snaps back to the status quo: Who copied from whom? From this point on, nothing is tested or proved; everything is simply the product of circular reasoning. Conzelmann and Lindemann illustrate this within their discussion of Mark 2:1–12: "From this question [Who copied from whom?] it then becomes clear: Mt abbreviates what seems to him as nonessential for the actual kernel of the narrative; the picturesque situation [found in Mark] bothers him; he seeks instead to emphasize more powerfully the didactic content."

What is set forth here as fact is nothing but fantasy formation. All that can be determined is that two concrete features found in Mark (2:2, 4) are lacking in Matthew. Since it has not been shown that Matthew used Mark, it is idle speculation to assert what mo-

19. Word counts are from the Greek text in Kurt Aland, *Synopsis Quattuor Evangeliorum* (Stuttgart: United Bible Society, 1975).

tives moved him to make changes. *The psychological plausibility of invented motives offers no proof that an event has taken place.* One could just as plausibly invent motives that explain why Mark made changes to Matthew in this passage. Both attempts lead nowhere. It is time to hold fast to the facts, instead of immediately explaining away the weight and significance of indisputable data with fantasy.

Conzelmann and Lindemann continue: "An astonishing proof for literary dependence is the agreement in the sentence construction found in Mt [9] v.[erse] 6/Mk [2] v. 10: in both places one finds *anacoluthon*."[20]

That is neither proof nor astonishing, for who can exclude with certainty the possibility that Jesus spoke in broken fashion here and that this is preserved in the Greek representations of his expression?

Again, Conzelmann and Lindemann say, "The comparison between [Matthew and Luke] is simple; the differences are—in Luke's sense—improvements." That is more circular reasoning. One can only improve on a source if that source is known—but that, once again, is precisely the question to be answered: Did Luke have a manuscript of Mark?

Conzelmann and Lindemann further state: "On the other hand, however, it is precisely [Luke 5] v. 21 that shows that Luke had the text of Mark before him. For in v. 21 Luke, like Mark, uses *grammateis* (and not, as one might have expected from Luke's usage in 5:17, *nomodidaskaloi*)" (see Mark 2:6).

Could Luke only have used the word in 5:21 if Mark furnished it for him in 2:6? Could he not have varied his usage independently of Mark? The only word in this verse that is identical right down to the inflection in Luke and Mark is *kai* (*and*). Mark uses thirteen words at that point to communicate what Luke says in twenty. Is that an indication of literary dependence?

Conzelmann and Lindemann claim to test the tenability of their hypothesis with a second pericope, the parable of the mustard seed (Mark 4:30–32). Here the data are, as the authors them-

20. [An *anacoluthon* is a syntactical irregularity. One thought is left incomplete as the speaker or writer shifts to another construction. In effect, Jesus abruptly interrupts his own explanation of why he has absolved the paralyzed man of his sins as he commands the man to get up and walk.]

selves admit, "considerably more complicated than in the first case [Mark 2:1–12]: Mark and Luke differ; Matthew seems to follow Mark against Luke, but also Luke against Mark. These data, too, are most readily accounted for by assuming Marcan priority."

This attempted explanation, however, is not so straightforward as their assertion suggests. The authors must introduce two additional hypothesis in order to complete the process they envision: (1) Luke made use, not of Mark, but of a tradition independent of Mark, and (2) Matthew attempted "to bring together both understandings, without however managing to arrive at an actual balance between them."

That is no proof for the assumption that Mark was a source for Matthew and Luke; it is rather the declaration of that assumption's bankruptcy. Before one sets up hypotheses, one should take note of the facts and ask whether they speak in favor of literary dependence:

> Of fifty-seven words in Mark 4:30–32, eight (14.03 percent) are identical in all three Synoptics.
>
> Of the remaining forty-nine words, Mark shares nine with Matthew and six with Luke.
>
> Mark, therefore, shares seventeen words with Matthew, or 29.82 percent of the total, and fourteen words with Luke, or 24.56 percent of the total.

Koester

In another standard textbook in New Testament study, *Introduction to the New Testament*, vol. 2: *History and Literature of Early Christianity*,[21] Helmut Koester notes in the "General Remarks" portion of a section entitled "Literary Criticism": "Only a small portion of the writings of the NT and other early Christian literature can be viewed as the single product of an individual author. All these writings had literary prototypes which influenced their shape; most of them used sources which determined their contents and forms to a large degree; many are not even preserved in their original form, but only in later redactions, editions, and compilations."[22]

21. Philadelphia: Fortress, 1982.
22. Ibid., 43.

That is a blanket assertion presented to the (student) reader as a presentation of securely established facts. It contains a series of implications, represented as unquestioned truths, although they are unprovable:

1. New Testament writings are the product of literary activity. Their primary frame of reference cannot be historical.
2. *Only a few* are the product of an individual author.
3. *All* had literary prototypes.
4. *Most* used sources.
5. *Many* are not preserved in their original form but were later reworked or compiled.

The reader who is not in a position to know better is grossly manipulated by this series of blanket assertions. The entire New Testament is reduced to a collection of secondary literary compositions, all of which had literary prototypes. This is how budding theologians and pastors are presented God's revelation, the Word of the Creator of heaven and earth, the proclamation of all-sufficient redemption in Jesus Christ. It is remarkable that church leaders wonder why pastors lack missionary vision and competence. Why should they put themselves out to spread secondary literary compositions among the people?

Zimmermann

Yet another textbook for New Testament study, *Neutestamentliche Methodenlehre*[23] by Heinrich Zimmermann, states that both "the content of the Synoptics itself, as well as an overview of the history of research, sufficiently demonstrate that extraordinary difficulties stand in the way of a solution to the Synoptic problem. There is no easy answer to so many complicated questions. Nevertheless, the attempt can be made to bring together observations that may be regarded as certain."[24] What does Zimmermann see as "observations that may be regarded as certain"?

"It is certain that the Synoptic gospels represent the end stage of a long process of development," he writes. But that is neither an observation, nor is it certain. It is simply asserted, without

23. 7th ed., revised by Klaus Kliesch, 1982.
24. Ibid., 81–82. All of the following quotations of Zimmermann are from these pages.

bringing forth even the hint of a proof. What is meant by "a long process of development"?

"A first stage of tradition formation already set in soon after the death and resurrection of Jesus. The eye-witnesses were bearers of the tradition and as such [were] guardians of it, . . ."

This statement is ambiguous. If the eye-witnesses were bearers and guardians of the tradition, in what sense can one speak of tradition formation? The eyewitnesses passed on, surely, what they had seen and heard. Yet Zimmermann's next, related assertion moves from being ambiguous to being utterly incomprehensible: "What form the first tradition assumed, and what alterations it might have been subjected to from the beginning, can only be determined, to a greater or lesser degree, by inference from the later forms with which we are familiar."

Without any stated justification it is here asserted that what the eyewitnesses passed along was not preserved intact. It was "subjected to alterations" and "can only be determined, to a greater or lesser degree, by inference. . . ." Zimmermann's subsequent statement of incapacity, "We can know nothing for sure," is absurd. The eyewitnesses did not disappear from the scene in a flash after two decades. A good number of them are highly likely to have survived until the second half of the A.D. 70s, or well beyond the time span during which Zimmermann thinks the Synoptics took final form. Someone who was 25 or 30 in A.D. 30 would have been 60 or 65 by A.D. 65. By that time a multitude of disciples, however, some of whom had known Jesus personally, would have heard with their own ears that which was presented with eyewitness authority. Who at that time would have dared to alter the "first tradition" beyond recognition?

Zimmermann continues: "A second stage of the tradition history is characterized by the formation of numerous smaller literary collections. This is supported by how Matthew and Luke demonstrably rely on written sources (cf. Luke 1:1–4). Here we must speak of a sayings collection, called Q, whose existence cannot be doubted. . . . To these written sources belongs also Mark's gospel, which both Matthew and Luke used as a source."

Zimmermann has unfortunately lost the ability, normally inculcated when one learns mathematics, to distinguish between assertion, presupposition, and proof. He offers his student readers assertions as if they were facts. Presupposing that Matthew and Luke are based on Q and Mark does not prove that there was a stage when numerous smaller literary collections developed. One cannot deduce from Luke 1:1–4 the proof that Matthew and Luke used written sources—certainly not in Matthew's case, and not even in Luke's either. Even if one wishes to understand Luke 1:1–2 as stating that Luke knew other gospel writings, one can still not infer from verses 2 and 3 that he made a source into the foundation of his presentation.

Further, one is quite justified in doubting the existence of Q. It is merely a hypothetical document for whose existence conclusive proof still has yet to be advanced. That Mark was the source behind Matthew and Luke is not a fact, despite what Zimmermann tries to get his readers to believe, but simply a hypothesis that still awaits thorough examination against all the relevant data of the Gospels.

"To the third stage of the tradition belong our three Synoptic gospels." Does this mean Mark's Gospel arose simultaneously in both the second and third stages?

"If the first stage lasted at least two decades, and if the transition to the second stage was not yet totally completed by the A.D. 50s, then the second half of the A.D. 60s will have been the decisive period for the rise of the Synoptic gospels."

Here one can trace how from each hypothesis a subsequent hypothesis is derived—while not one of them has seen the light of rigorous testing:

1. *Hypothesis presupposition*: "There were three stages." This is totally unsubstantiated. Zimmermann admits the stages cannot be clearly demarcated when he writes, "[A]s the rich store of material in both Matthew and Luke shows, the first stage persisted along with the second and then extended into the third."
2. *Hypothesis continuation*: "This stage lasted at least two decades." That is a free-floating assertion, for which no argument is advanced.
3. *Hypothesis inference*: So "the second half of the A.D. 60s will have been the decisive period for the rise of the Synoptic gospels."

Imaginary stages are arbitrarily assigned time spans, and the result is a fictitious dating of the Synoptic Gospels. Then the claim is made that a rigorous "methodology for New Testament interpretation" is being passed along.

That's how scientific "scientific theology" is.

Is There Literary Dependence among the Synoptic Gospels?

Introduction to Part 2

In part 1 we saw that the Synoptic problem was not discovered through a thorough an investigation of the Gospels. Its "solutions" should be regarded as somewhat whimsical speculations rather than scientific results. The form and manner in which subsequent generations were familiarized with the "problem" and its "solution" certainly do not deserve to be called science. Research does more than set up hypotheses as a foundation on which to work. Science does not meet every difficulty with the invention of additional hypotheses. Certainly, by using such a method one can demonstrate the internal consistency of one's thought, but that alone is not scientific work. Admittedly, in the humanities hypotheses do not always readily admit to empirical testing. Nevertheless, one can at least carefully and thoroughly consult the relevant data, thereby discerning whether those data speak against or for the hypothesis in question. It is no adequate test if a preferred hypothesis wins a technical victory in comparison with other hypotheses. That amounts to nothing more than proving the superiority of one hypothesis to its rivals, which is circular reasoning. In the humanities, a scientific examination of a hypothesis must consult all relevant data. The hypothesis must be subjected to rigorous debate. Alternate possibilities cannot be dismissed in a priori, discriminatory fashion. Whether such alternate possibilities are "uncritical" or appropriate must be the result of the investigation. Prejudgments do not befit scientific inquiry.

It is, accordingly, time to attempt a fresh investigation of the so-called *Synoptic problem* and its solution.

Search for an Answer

The Synoptic problem, as historical-critial theology understands it, was defined by Rudolf Bultmann as "the problem of literary dependence" among the Synoptic Gospels that arises because of their similarities and differences. A form of literary dependence is also assumed to exist if "the root of the three gospels is an orally forumulated proto-gospel."[1] If this problem is approached on the basis of all the relevant data available in the Gospels, rather than on the basis of preconceived hypotheses, then the primary task is first to *clarify whether investigation of the data yields sufficient reason for positing the likelihood of literary dependence.*

In other words, before the question, "What is the nature of the literary dependence?" is discussed, we must ask, "Is there literary dependence among the Synoptic Gospels?"

The question must be placed objectively. There must be openness to either an affirmative or a negative answer, assuming that the answer proceeds from the data. *No answer can be rejected as uncritical at the outset. Only the data can demand a yes-or-no decision.*

This point must be emphasized in view of the heavy burden a "no" to this question would have to bear. Should investigation

1. Georg Strecker and Udo Schnelle, *Einführung in die neutestamentliche Exegese*, 2d ed. (Göttingen, 1985), 48. Translation by Robert Yarbrough.

of the data disprove literary dependence among the Synoptics, one of the supporting pillars of New Testament criticism (or "science," as it is called in some quarters) collapses. Without the two-source theory, form criticism has no basis, for "the history of the Synoptic tradition" was based on the two-source theory. This theory presupposed the need to distinguish between tradition and redaction. Material common to the three Gospels was explained as tradition; material unique to one Gospel, if a whole pericope was not involved, was explained as redaction. Even differentiation between a phase of oral tradition and the subsequent phase of reducing to written form (*Verschriftlichung*) as Gospels stands or falls with the assumption of their literary dependence.

Tradition, Redaction, and Dependence

Strangely, no one noticed that differentiating between tradition and redaction contradicts the assumption of literary dependence. For literary dependence means that both tradition and the redaction of Mark must have lain before Matthew and Luke. Where Matthew and Luke diverge from Mark in introducing pericopes and transitional material before and between pericopes, this must have involved conscious, new editorial work. It could not reflect that the same tradition had been filtered through contrasting settings. Dependence assumes that the writers of Matthew and Luke used newly created introductions and transitions.

The logical consequence was drawn in redaction-critical research, but not its implications for attempts to differentiate between what is tradition and what is redaction. Matthew and Luke were implicitly assumed to be able to differentiate between tradition and redaction in Mark and to have determined to alter mainly the redactional portions.

The whole domain of New Testament criticism that concerns itself with investigating the Synoptic Gospels rests on a dual presupposition: the Synoptic problem and an assumption regarding how to solve it. Should it turn out that there is no literary dependence among the Synoptic Gospels, then the rug is pulled out from under about 40 percent of New Testament research as it is carried on within historical-critical circles. That cannot hinder us, however, from considering the question objectively and conscientiously in the light of the data.

The agreement in content among the first three Gospels is striking. We will try to go into more detail concerning its extent in chapter 3. This agreement in content—the fact that, to no small extent, the same pericopes occur in Matthew, Mark and Luke—has until now always been chalked up as the result of literary dependence. That is, however, methodologically impermissible. For objective consideration must admit that agreement in content can have either of two causes. The agreement may have passed from one literary work to another, or it may have been passed along for historical reasons.

Certainly *literary dependence* is apt to result in agreement in content. But it is not only literary productions derived from a common written source that evince such agreements. Independent reports of the same *historical events* do precisely the same thing. Any who doubt this need only compare different newspaper articles on the same athletic contest, or eyewitness descriptions of the same traffic accident, or school essays about something the whole class saw. Unless one prejudicially, in a priori fashion, excludes the possibility of explanation by historical factors—and such an exclusion would have to be called unscientific bias—one cannot automatically use agreement in content as an argument for literary dependence. One must consider the dependence only in the abstract: Whether agreement in content is literarily or historically transmitted can only be decided after determining whether literary dependence exists.

An Investigation of the Data

Literary dependence can only be proven or disproven from the actual wording; one must restrict study to the linguistic data. Here it will not do to point to individual formulaic agreements encompassing just a sentence, or even a half sentence or just a few words. Such a practice often obscures the fact that there is no real contextual conformity at all from a linguistic point of view. Agreement in individual formulations does not automatically show literary dependence. That kind of clarity can be attained only after a general and thoroughgoing investigation of all data. The extent of agreement, as well as the differences, must be understood quantitatively if one wishes to come to an objective, well-grounded result. It is not enough to quantify by verses, which has been done, since considerable differences are found within parallel verses when one scrutinizes the actual wording rather than simply the general content. The basis for quantification should be the word as the smallest component of meaning. The respective lengths of various words should not be considered, for they counterbalance themselves on the average.

Obviously an investigation of the above description must work from the Greek text; specifically I have chosen to use Kurt Aland's *Synopsis Quattuor Evangeliorum*. In order to avoid unnecessary complication in our study I have accepted without discussion Aland's text-critical decisions and pericope divisions. We have also consulted Robert Morgenthaler's *Die Statistik des neutestamentlichen Wortschatzes*. Many of the statistical calculations below are my own; they have been generated by traditional means, not by computer. The reasons for this are personal rather than material. Of course one can check my figures by computer. Yet one should note that experts calculate the margin of error for relevant computer programs to be as high as 2 percent. While I cannot rule out the possibility of an occasional error, I would like to think that repeated checking will hold the percent of error to a considerably lower level than that. We are dealing here with a methodologically new starting point, and no one will achieve perfect results the first time through. I will gladly receive corrections.

In my investigation I restrict myself to the material common to Matthew, Mark, and Luke. The same methodological procedure also applies to material common to Matthew and Luke; I have proven this in a number of test passages.

The material common to Matthew, Mark, and Luke must be examined in several steps to ascertain whether literary dependence exists:

1. *The composition of Matthew and Luke will be determined quantitatively.* This will establish the extent of material common to Mark found in Matthew and Luke, respectively, and to Matthew and Luke as compared with Luke (chapter 3).
2. *I will clarify whether one can establish an index for the literary dependence of the three synoptic gospels,* based on the com-

monalities in the narrative sequence—the so-called *Ako-luthia* or common thread of tradition (chapter 4).

3. *An investigation "lengthwise," so to speak (as opposed to a cross-section) will calculate the extent of parallelism between Mathew, Mark, and Luke in relation to the Marcan material.* First, I will compute the extent of common pericopes; second I will determine the extent of commonality within the pericopes. This second step will measure or quantify the differences within the scope of common pericopes (chapter 5).

4. *Another quantitative comparison of Synoptic pericopes will investigate the extent of agreement or difference in the actual wording of every single pericope which Matthew, Mark, and Luke have in common.* Combined with this will be investigation of cross-sections which show the average extent of agreement among the parallel pericopes (chapter 6).

5. *An examination of vocabulary will complete this comparison.* If Mark was the source for Matthew and Luke, then one would assume that Mark's vocabulary is reduplicated, if not entirely then at least substantially, in the later books (chapter 7).

Since the two-source hypothesis has been established in continental Europe and far beyond, the five steps above are designed to closely relate to this hypothesis. In principle, however, the results could be applied just as well to the Griesbach theory or any other theory of literary dependence. In summarizing the results the central question—whether the data collected in the five steps support the idea of literary dependendence among the three Synoptic Gospels—will finally be answered. I will also discuss the consequences of these data for both the two-source and the Griesbach theories, respectively.

It should be pointed out, finally, that these are *research methods.* No one should burden beginning theologians with the expectation that they construct a quantitative comparison of the Synoptics as part of sermon preparation, or that they undertake exhaustive vocabularly investigations.

I have done this work as a labor of love in two respects. First, some readers have been ensnared in a historical-critical mode of thinking that disguises itself as science; I would like to show them how a work ought to look that meets the just requirements of "science" in the area of synoptic research. Second, I would like to help free evangelicals from their fascination with the alleged scientific character of historical-critical interpretation of the Bible. I want them to discover their own interpretative path. This new path should no longer be just a narrow side-trail in the historical-critical direction. This path finally must be delivered from the tendency to remain so concerned with historical-critical discussion that one's vision is constantly overshadowed by it and one's findings dominated by reaction to it.

These chapters and the research undergirding them are an *opus alienum*, a strange undertaking. Normally I do not handle God's Word by counting words instead of being edified by what the words say. I have been driven to this, however, by the dreadful effect of historical-critical theology, not least in its championing of the Synoptic problem, which is its cornerstone.

By diligently performing the necessary drudgery I want to clear away the rubbish heaps of hypotheses that have denied access to God's Word and cast doubt on its veracity.

May the love of Christ which has driven me in my efforts be palpable in this work.

3

The Composition
of Matthew and Luke

The question of the composition of Matthew and Luke is not integral to research centering on the literary dependence of the Synoptics. It is a question that should be answered in passing, however, to recognize the role played by the material the two hold in common with Mark and with each other.

To establish the composition of the gospels of Matthew and Luke we must distinguish three entities:

1. material unique to Matthew and to Luke;
2. material common to Matthew and Mark and to Luke and Mark, and
3. material common to all three

The concept of *common material* arises from comparison with *unique material*; unique material appears in only one book, while two or more Gospels share common material. The concept only makes an observation from the data and implies no assumption regarding origin. Sometimes one must distinguish between common material and unique material within the same pericope. There is, very rarely, unique material in a pericope of Luke or Matthew that is surrounded by material shared with Mark. More often material unique to Matthew or Luke appears in a passage the two Gospels have in common with one another.

Although such unique material is counted as part of the minor additional details,[1] still one must distinguish, at least in principle, what is common from what is unique. Not every minor additional detail should be counted as unique, but only that which possesses its own content, formally independent content not found in parallel accounts. In a few cases, whether a segment should be counted as unique material or merely as minor additional detail is obviously a judgment call.

Points of contact in the content or similarities in individual linguistic formulations are insufficient grounds for declaring a pericope to be common material. The "poor in spirit" in Matthew's Sermon on the Mount (5:3) are not the same as the "poor" in Luke's Sermon on the Plain (6:20–26)—in Luke the poor are expressly set over against the rich. Similarly, the anointing of Luke 7:36–50 is too different in specific details to qualify as a parallel to Mark 14:3–9. The two genealogies of Jesus (Matthew 1 and Luke 3) are counted as unique, rather than as somehow common, material.

Some of what is normally attributed to the sayings source (Q) appears in my classification as unique material, because calling it common material presupposes that there is a parallel. Only a true parallel counts, not a hypothetical assignment to a source on the basis of a formal structure or direct proximity to verses that are common material.

The material common to Matthew and Luke must be tallied separately for either Gospel, since the parallel passages diverge from each other in different directions in their minor additional details.

The material unique to Matthew and Luke, along with their common material, is itemized in figures 3.1–3.3. These presentations certainly may need correcting in details, and different individuals might reach slightly different numbers; the overall results, however, will probably not prove to be very far wide of the mark. The results need here to be recorded and assessed:

1. Hans-Herbert Stoldt, *History and Criticism of the Marcan Hypothesis* (Macon, Ga.: Mercer University Press, 1960), 11–18.

Matthew

The material unique to Matthew comprises 4729 words, or 25.87 percent of the total number of words in Matthew (Fig. 3.1).

The material common to Matthew and Luke, counting the words as they appear in Matthew, amounts to 3412 words, or 18.17 percent of Matthew (Fig. 3.2).

Therefore, 8141 of Matthew's words do not appear in Mark, or 44.54 percent of the total number of words in Matthew.

Matthew's material shared with Mark can be calculated by subtracting this sum from the total number of words in Matthew

Figure 3.1

Material Unique to Matthew

1:2–17 = 217 words	10:22b–23 = 36	19:10–12 = 62
1:18–25 = 162	10:40–41 = 31	20:1–16 = 240
2:1–12 = 220	11:28–30 = 45	21:14–16 = 61
2:13–21 = 195	12:5–7 = 44	21:28–32 = 104
2:22–23 = 42	12:36 = 30	23:2–3 = 32
5:3–10 = 72	13:24–30 = 138	23:5 = 20
5:16 = 23	13:36–43 = 152	23:8–12 = 60
5:17–20 = 101	13:44–46 = 54	23:15–22 = 145
5:21–24 = 95	13:47–50 = 72	25:1–12 = 170
5:27–28 = 25	13:51–52 = 32	25:31–46 = 279
5:33–37 = 82	14:28–31 = 87	26:52–54 = 47
6:1–4 = 92	15:12–13 = 29	27:3–10 = 118
6:5–6 = 65	16:16b–19 = 86	27:19 = 27
6:7–8 = 34	17:24–27 = 100	27:24–25 = 44
6:16–18 = 63	18:3b–4 = 36	27:51b–53 = 37
7:6 = 25	18:10 = 27	27:62–66 = 83
7:15 = 16	18:15–18 = 87	28:2–4 = 46
7:21–23 = 67	18:19–20 = 44	28:9–10 = 37
9:27–33 = 75	18:23–35 = 213	28:11–15 = 73
10:5–6 = 30	**Total: 4729 words (25.87 percent of Matthew)**	

Figure 3.2

Material Common to Matthew and Luke

Matthew	Luke
3:7–10 = 75 words	3:7–9 = 72 words
3:12 = 26	3:17 = 25
4:1–12 = 183	4:1–13 = 203
5:11–12 = 35	6:22–23 = 51
5:25–26 = 43	12:58–59 = 49
5:32 = 22	16:18 = 17
5:38–42 = 69	6:29–30 = 40
5:43–48 = 95	6:27–28, 32–36 = 115
6:9–15 = 91	11:2–4 = 44
6:19–21 = 49	12:33–34 = 36
6:22–23 = 45	11:34–36 = 63
6:24 = 27	16:13 = 28
6:25–34 = 186	12:22–32 = 175
7:3–5 = 64	6:41–42 = 70
7:7–11 = 74	11:9–13 = 75
7:12 = 23	6:31 = 11
7:13–14 = 44	13:23–24 = 29
7:16–17 = 29	6:43–44 = 34
7:24–27 = 95	6:47–49 = 83
8:5–13 = 165	7:1–10 = 186
10:26–33 = 137	12:2–9 = 146
10:34–36 = 42	12:51–53 = 57
10:37–38 = 38	14:25–27 = 62
11:2–4 = 63	7:18–23 = 102
11:7–11 = 94	7:24–28 = 94
11:16–19 = 65	7:31–35 = 76
11:20–24 = 93	10:12–15 = 63
11:25–27 = 69	10:21–22 = 74
12:27–29 = 37	11:19–20 = 37
12:43–45 = 68	11:24–26 = 74
13:16–17 = 36	10:23–26 = 38
13:33 = 23	13:20–21 = 24
18:12–13 = 48	15:4–6 = 57
18:21–22 = 32	17:4 = 17
22:1–14 = 223	14:15–24 = 180
23:4 = 20	11:46 = 24
23:23–36 = 260	11:39–42, 44–51 = 186
23:37–39 = 55	13:34–35 = 53

24:27–28 = 28	17:24–37b = 37
24:37–44 = 129	17:26, 27, 30, 34, 35; 12:39–40 = 111
24:45–51 = 111	12:41–46 = 121
25:14–30 = 301	19:11–27 = 281

Total: 3412 words shared with Luke (18.17 percent of Matt.)   **3320 words shared with Matthew (17.11 percent of Luke)**

Figure 3.3

Material Unique to Luke

1:5–23 = 378 words	11:5–8 = 86	17:20–21 = 38
1:26–38 = 208	11:27–28 = 39	17:28–29 = 29
1:39–56 = 232	12:13–15 = 54	18:1–8 = 138
1:57–80 = 326	12:16–21 = 94	18:9–14 = 117
2:1–7 = 104	12:47–48 = 48	19:1–10 = 147
2:8–20 = 208	12:49 = 13	19:41–44 = 73
2:21–38 = 310	12:54–56 = 46	21:21b–22 = 39
2:41–52 = 196	13:1–9 = 169	21:24 = 21
3:10–14 = 73	13:10–17 = 160	21:25b–26a = 22
3:23–38 = 164	13:22–30 = 129	21:18 = 15
4:16–30 = 279	13:31–33 = 56	21:34–56 = 57
5:1–11 = 207	14:1–6 = 82	21:37–38 = 31
6:20b–21 = 22	14:7–14 = 154	22:15–16 = 33
6:24–26 = 43	14:28–33 = 102	22:31–32 = 31
7:11–17 = 126	15:8–10 = 53	22:35–38 = 79
7:36–50 = 274	15:11–32 = 342	23:4–12 = 157
8:1–3 = 62	16:1–9 = 188	23:13–16 = 60
9:52–56 = 55	16:10–12 = 46	23:27–31 = 81
9:61–62 = 40	16:14–15 = 38	23:39–43 = 72
10:17–20 = 74	16:19–31 = 244	24:13–35 = 331
10:29–37 = 156	17:7–10 = 68	24:36–43 = 86
10:38–42 = 95	17:11–19 = 116	24:44–53 = 142

Total: 7758 words (39.98 percent of Luke)

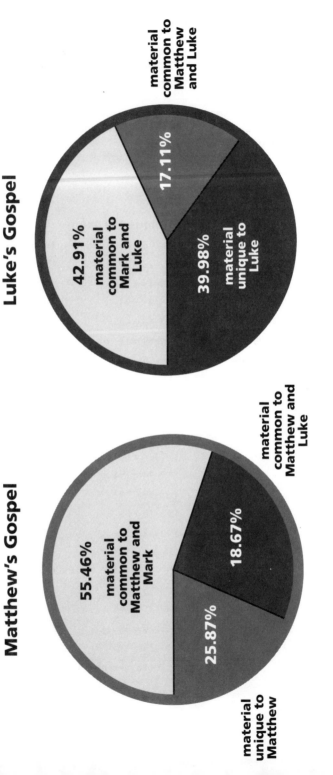

Figure 3.4. The Composition of Matthew and Luke

Matthew's Gospel

55.46% material common to Matthew and Mark

25.87%

18.67%

material common to Matthew and Luke

material unique to Matthew

Luke's Gospel

material common to Matthew and Luke

17.11%

42.91% material common to Mark and Luke

39.98% material unique to Luke

(18,278 as counted by R. Morgenthaler[2]). Material common to Matthew and Mark amounts to 10,137 words or 55.46 percent of the words Matthew contains.

The material that Matthew has in common with Mark is, therefore, something over half his Gospel. This Matthew-Mark common material is a good 10 percent more than the material unique to Matthew, together with the Matthew-Luke common material.

Luke

The composition of Luke's Gospel looks different.

Figure 3.3 shows that Luke's unique material amounts to 7758 words (3008 more words than in Matthew), or 39.98 percent of all the words Luke contains (19,404, according to Morgenthaler[3]).

The material in Luke, in common with Matthew, amounts to 3320 words, or 17.11 percent of the words Luke contains (Fig. 3.2). This is still less than half of Luke's unique material (7758 unique; 3320 shared with Matthew).

That leaves 8326 words of Luke that are shared with Mark, or 42.91 percent of the total number of words Luke contains.

By comparison, this is only 2.93 percent more than Luke's unique material (7758 unique; 8326 shared with Mark).

In round numbers, Matthew shares 55 percent of its content with Mark. Luke, on the other hand, shares only 43 percent of its content with Mark. That is a difference of 12 percent between Matthew and Luke. Figure 3.4 presents the overall picture.

Later we will draw some conclusions from all of these data. For now, let us put them aside and turn to the order of the Synoptic narratives.

2. Robert Morgenthaler, *Statistik des neutestamentlichen Wortschatzes* (Zurich-Frankfurt: Gotthelf, 1958), 164.
3. Ibid.

4

Commonality in the Narrative Thread of the Synoptic Gospels

One of the chief arguments for literary dependence among the Synoptics is thought to be the similar order of their narrative material, the so-called *akoluthia* (from Gk. *akoloutheō*: "follow," or "go behind"). Literary dependence is considered to be firmly established by the observation that there appears not only the same narratives, but even a similar order in their arrangement.

Against this a fundamental objection must be lodged: Common sequence in narrative by no means necessitates the use of the same literary source; it can also arise when several persons independently report the same succession of events. Similar narrative sequence thus can be attributed to either of two causes: (1) transmission through a common literary source; (2) the nature and progression of events described.

In historical-critical theology, the second possibility is totally ignored or dismissed at the outset as "uncritical." Only the first possibility receives attention. Is that because the critic does not wish to allow the gospel reports to be seen as a sequence of events? Does the critic, because of this personal bias, adopt an approach that contradicts the clear testimony, not only of the three Synoptics, but of all four Gospels? Is the insistence on literary dependence in the narrative sequence perhaps grounded in the critic's *a priori* decision not to see the gospels as true-to-fact descriptions, even though they correspond to the pattern of histories of the ancient "lives" of famous persons? Obviously the Gospels are not "biography" in the sense that became accepted in the nineteenth century, but no true historian would take this as a standard for something written in the first century.[1]

The Extent of Parallel Sequence

Although similarity in narrative sequence in itself falls short of proving a literary dependence, this question needs to be pursued: Can one discover in Matthew and Luke a common narrative thread that is identical to the narrative sequence of Mark? Hans-Herbert Stoldt already answered this question when he said that "nowhere does the Gospel of Mark appear in the other two Gospels as an intact and continuous narrative; rather, it runs parallel to the others, always only temporarily and partially, in changing intervals and in quite different lengths. Sometimes it

1. See Wolfgang Schadewaldt, "*Die Zuverlässigkeit der synoptischen Tradition*," *Theologische Beiträge* 13 (1982): 201–23; esp. 222–23:
    When one notes this tendency, say in the essays of [Ernst] Käsemann, then one sees that this concept of the historical Jesus is determined first by facticity, positive facticity, second by causality, third through a leveling plausibility, fourth through psychologizing, and fifth through inner development. All five of these concepts, applied to someone like Plutarch, would disqualify him from having written biography. For antiquity constructed its biographies in wonderfully clear fashion, not on the basis of causality, plausibility, and inner development, which are categories of the 19th century, but rather on two things: *pragmata* and *logoi* [deeds and words], *ta prachthenta kai ta lechtenta* [the things done and the things said]. And in my judgment they were correct. When one rightly apprehends the occurrences, and most of all the situation, i.e. the occurrences in their context, as well as the *logoi*, then one is in the best position to say what can be said only about a historical phenomenon. The manner in which one gives form to the *pragmata* and *logoi* is the trademark of the noble biographers: that is how they operated. And one must, I believe, go on to say that [Rudolf] Bultmann and others rationalized these things in 19th century fashion, gave them form in the moralistic manner of liberalism—and then opposed them. But they did not oppose them in the sense of opposing a method, but rather as opposing the Word of Scripture. What was thereby destroyed, in that the historical Jesus was destroyed, is nothing other than that which lives inviolably in the Gospel: the person of the Lord himself.

runs parallel to Matthew for a passage, sometimes to Luke, sometimes to both, occasionally to neither. Insofar as all three do not coincide, the parallelism of one of them to Mark ceases as soon as it begins with the other."[2]

I wish to furnish further corroboration to what Stoldt has established through quantification. Fig. 4.1, *Akoluthia* plots out my findings.

Commonalities in All Three Synoptics

According to my reckoning, based on Kurt Aland's "Conspectus locorum parallelorum evangeliorum,"[3] Mark consists of 115 separate sections.[4] Of these 115 sections, only fifty-eight appear in all three Synoptics in the same sequence, or around 50.43 percent. That is no more than half!

Of these fifty-eight sections, no fewer than twenty-one (36.21 percent) relate to Christ's death and resurrection—more than one-third, although passion and resurrection narratives in Mark amount to a total of just twenty-four units out of 115, or 20.87 percent. Of the twenty-four sections relating to the passion and resurrection in Mark,[5] twenty-one occur in the same sequence in all the Synoptics (87.50 percent).

Now, surely no one will wish to deny that the order of the passion and resurrection accounts has objective grounds: the cross-examination cannot be reported until after the arrest; the crucifixion cannot be reported until after the sentencing; the resurrection cannot be reported until after the burial. Therefore, to be precise, only the Synoptic agreement in narrative sequences outside the passion and resurrection accounts can be relevant to the

2. Hans-Herbert Stoldt, *History and Criticism of the Marcan Hypothesis* (Macon, Ga.: Mercer University Press, 1980), 136.

3. Kurt Aland, *Synopsis Quattuor Evangeliorum* (Stuttgart: United Bible Society, 1975), 551–75.

4. Not including Mark 1:1 and 16:9–20, the so-called "longer ending of Mark," which I by no means think is spurious, but regarding which I do not wish here to enter into a discussion.

At one point I depart from Aland. As a parallel to Mark 11:11 he gives Matt. 21:10–17. In my view the only parallels here are Mark 11:11a/Matt. 21:10a and Mark 11:11b/Matt. 21:17. Matt. 21:10b–16 does not belong in the category of a parallel. Thus I arrive at two sections (70a and 70b) and come to 115 total rather than 114.

5. Mark 14:1–16:8.

Figure 4.1 Akoluthia: Narrative Sequence between Mark and Matthew

Divisions of pericopes follow the "Conspectus Locorum parallelorum evangeliorum" in Kurt Aland, *Synopsis Quattuor Evangeliorum* (Stuttgart: Deutsche Bibelstiftung, 1978), 551–575.

+   Akoluthia (hypothesized original Marcan narrative order allegedly followed by Matthew and Luke)
−   Missing from Matthew or not in Akoluthia
X   not in Akoluthia
C   Material not in Mark but common to Matthew and Luke
UMt Material not in Mark and unique to Matthew

Sequence of pericopes in Mark, according to Aland's *Synopsis*	Matthean pericopes according to Aland's *Synopsis*	Sequence of pericopes in Mark, according to Aland's *Synopsis*	Matthean pericopes according to Aland's *Synopsis*
1. + 1:1	+ 1:1 C 1:2–2:23 (5 Matt. pericopes)	17. − 2:13–17	−
		18. − 2:18–22	−
2. + 1:2–6	+ 3:1–6 C 3:7–10 (1 Matt. pericope)	19. − 2:23–28	−
		20. − 3:1–6	−
3. + 1:7–8	+ 3:11–12	21. − 3:7–12	− C and/or UMt 4:24–7:29; (27 Matt. pericopes) − or X or C and/or UMt 8:1–12:21 (29 Matt. pericopes)
4. + 1:9–11	+ 3:13–17		
5. + 1:12–13	+ 4:1–11		
6. + 1:14a	+ 4:12		
7. + 1:14b–15	+ 4:13–17	22. − 3:13–19a	−
8. + 1:16–20	+ 4:18–22	23. − 3:19b–21	−
9. − 1:21–22	−	24. + 3:22–27	+ 12:22–30
10. − 1:23–28	−	25. + 3:28–30	+ 12:31–37 UMt 12:38–45 (2 Matt. pericopes)
11. − 1:29–31	−		
12. − 1:32–34	−	26. + 3:31–35	+ 12:46–50
13. − 1:35–38	−	27. + 4:1–9	+ 13:1–9
14. + 1:39	+ 4:23	28. + 4:10–12	+ 13:10–17
15. − 1:40–45	−	29. + 4:13–20	+ 13:18–23
16. − 2:1–12	−	30. − 4:21–25	−

Sequence of pericopes in Mark, according to Aland's *Synopsis*	Matthean pericopes according to Aland's *Synopsis*	Sequence of pericopes in Mark, according to Aland's *Synopsis*	Matthean pericopes according to Aland's *Synopsis*
31. − 4:26–29	– UMt 13:24–30 (1 Matt. pericope)	57. + 9:14–29	+ 17:14–21
		58. + 9:30–32	+ 17:22–23 UMt 17:24–27 (1 Matt. pericope)
32. + 4:30–32	+ 13: 31–32 UMt 13:33 (1 Matt. pericope)	59. + 9:33–37	+ 18:1–5
		60. − 9:38–41	–
33. + 4:33–34	+ 13: 34–35 UMt 13:36–52 (4 Matt. pericopes)	61. + 9:42–50	+1 8:6–9 C 18:10–14 (1 Matt. pericope) UMt 18:15–35 (4 Matt. pericopes)
34. − 4:35–41	–		
35. − 5:1–20	–		
36. − 5:21–43	–	62. + 10: 1	+ 19:1–2
37. + 6:1–6a	13:53–58	63. + 10:2–12	+ 19:3–12
38. − 6:6b–13	–	64. + 10:13–16	+ 19:13–15
39. + 6:14–16	+ 14:1–2	65. + 10:17–22	+ 19:16–22
40. + 6:17–29	+ 14:3–12	66. + 10:23–31	+ 19:23–30 UMt 20:1–16 (1 Matt. pericope)
41. − 6:30–31	–		
42. + 6:32–44	+ 14:13–21	67. + 10:32–34	+ 20:17–19
43. + 6:45–52	+ 14:22–33	68. + 10:35–45	+ 20:20–28
44. + 6:53–56	+ 14:34–36	69. + 10:46–52	+ 20.29–34
45. + 7:1–23	+ 15:1–20	70. + 11:1–10	+ 21:1–9
46. + 7:24–30	+ 15:21–28	71a. + 11:11a	+ 21:10a X and UMt 21:10b–16 (1 Matt. pericope)
47. + 7:31–37	+ 15:29–31		
48. + 8:1–10	+ 15:32–39	71b. + 11:11b	+ 21:17
49. + 8:11–13	+ 16:1–4	72. + 11:12–14	+ 21:18–19
50. + 8:14–21	+ 16:5–12	73. − 11:15–17	–
51. − 8:22–26	–	74. − 11:18–19	–
52. + 8:27–30	+ 16:13–20	75. + 11:20–26	+ 21:20–22
53. + 8:31–33	+ 16:21–23	76. + 11:27–33	+ 21:23–27 UMt 21:28–32 (1 Matt. pericope)
54. + 8:34–9:1	+ 16:24–28		
55. + 9:2–10	+ 17:1–9		
56. + 9:11–13	+ 17:10–13		

Sequence of pericopes in Mark, according to Aland's *Synopsis*	Matthean pericopes according to Aland's *Synopsis*	Sequence of pericopes in Mark, according to Aland's *Synopsis*	Matthean pericopes according to Aland's *Synopsis*
77. + 12:1–12	+ 21:33–46 UMt 22:1–14 (1 Matt. pericope)	96. + 14:18–21	+ 26:21–25
		97. + 14:22–25	+ 26:26–29
78. + 12:13–17	+ 22:15–22	98. + 14:26–31	+ 26:30–35
79. + 12:18–27	+ 22:23–33	99. + 14:32–42	+ 26:36–46
80. + 12:28–34	+ 22:34–40	100. + 14:43–52	+ 26:47–56
81. + 12:35–37a	+ 22:41–46	101. + 14:53–65	+ 26:57–68
82. + 12:37b–40	+ 23:1–36 UMt 23:37–39 (1 Matt. pericope)	102. + 14:66–72	+ 26:69–75
		103. + 15:1	+ 27:1–2 UMt 27:3–10 (1 Matt. pericope)
83. – 12:41–44	–		
84. + 13:1–2	+ 24:1–2	104. + 15:2–5	+ 27:11–14
85. + 13:3–8	+ 24:3–8	105. + 15:6–14	+ 27:15–23
86. + 13:9–13	+ 24:9–14	106. + 15:15	+ 27:24–26
87. + 13:14–20	+ 24:15–22	107. + 15:16–20a	+ 27:27–31a
88. + 13:21–23	+ 24:23–28	108. + 15:20b–21	+ 27:31b–32
89. +13:24–27	+ 24:29–31	109. + 15:22–26	+ 27:33–37
90. + 13:28–32	+ 24:32–36	110. + 15:27–32a	+ 27:38–43
91. – 13:33–37	– C and/or UMt 24:37–2546 (5 Matt. pericopes)	111. + 15:32b	+ 27:44
		112. + 15:33–39	+ 27:45–54
		113. + 15:40–41	+ 27: 55–56
92. + 14:1–2	+ 26:1–5	114. + 15:42–47	+ 27:57–61 UMt 27:62–66 (1 Matt. pericope)
93. + 14:3–9	+ 26:6–13		
94. + 14:10–11	+ 26:14–16	115. + 16:1–8	+ 28:1–8
95. + 14:12–17	+ 26:17–20		

Akoluthia: Narrative Sequence between Mark and Luke

+   Akoluthia (hypothesized original Marcan narrative order allegedly followed by Matthew and Luke)

–   Missing from Luke or not in Akoluthia

X   not in Akoluthia

C   Material not in Mark but common to·Matthew and Luke

ULk   Material not in Mark and unique to Luke

Sequence of pericopes in Mark, according to Aland's *Synopsis*	Lucan pericopes according to Aland's *Synopsis*	Sequence of pericopes in Mark, according to Aland's *Synopsis*	Lucan pericopes according to Aland's *Synopsis*
1. ÷ 1:1	+ 1:1–4 C and ULk 1:5–2:52 (9 Lucan pericopes)	22. + 3:13–19a	+ 6:12–16 C and/or ULk 6:17–8:3 (13 Lucan pericopes)
2. + 1:2–6	+ 3:1–6 C 3:7–9 (1 Lucan pericope) ULk 3:10–14 (1 Lucan pericope)	23. − 3:19b–21	–
		24. + 3:22–27	–
		25. + 3:28–30	–
		26. + 3:31–35	–
3. + 1:7–8	+ 3:15–18 ULk 3:19–20 (1 Lucan pericope)	27. + 4:1–9	+ 8:4–8
		28. + 4:10–12	+ 8:9–10
4. + 1:9–11	+ 3:21–22 ULk 3:23–38 (1 Lucan pericope)	29. + 4:13–20	+ 8:11–15
		30. + 4:21–25	+ 8:16–18
5. + 1:12–13	+ 4:1–13	31. − 4:26–29	–
6. + 1:14a	+ 4:14a	32. − 4:30–32	–
7. + 1:14b–15	+ 4:14b–15 ULk 4:16–30 (1 Lucan pericope)	33. − 4:33–34	– X 8:19–21 (1 Lucan pericope)
8. − 1:16–20	–	34. + 4:35–41	+ 8:22–25
9. + 1:21–22	+ 4:31–32	35. + 5:1–20	+ 8:26–39
10. + 1:23 28	+ 4:33–37	36. + 5:21–43	+ 8:40–56
11. + 1:29–31	+ 4:38–39	37. − 6:1–6a	–
12. + 1:32–34	+ 4:40–41	38. + 6:6b–13	+ 9:1–6
13. + 1:35–38	+ 4:42–43	39. + 6:14–16	+ 9:7–9
14. + 1:39	+ 4:44 ULk 5:1–11 (1 Lucan pericope)	40. − 6:17–29	–
		41. + 6:30–31	+ 9:10a
15. + 1:40–45	+ 5:12–16	42. + 6:32–44	+ 9:10b–17
16. + 2:1–12	+ 5:17–26	43. − 6:45–52	–
17. + 2:13–17	+ 5:27–32	44. − 6:53–56	–
18. + 2:18–22	+ 5:33–39	45. − 7:1–23	–
19. + 2:23–28	+ 6:1–5	46. − 7:24–30	–
20. + 3:1–6	+ 6:6–11	47. − 7:31–37	–
21. − 3:7–12	–	48. − 8:1–10	–
		49. − 8:11–13	–

Sequence of pericopes in Mark, according to Aland's *Synopsis*	Lucan pericopes according to Aland's *Synopsis*	Sequence of pericopes in Mark, according to Aland's *Synopsis*	Lucan pericopes according to Aland's *Synopsis*
50. – 8:14–21	–	76. + 11:27–33	+ 20:1–8
51. – 8:22–26	–	77. + 12:1–12	+ 20:9–19
52. + 8:27–30	+ 9:18–21	78. + 12:13–17	+ 20:20–26
53. + 8:31–33	+ 9:22	79. + 12:18–27	+ 20:27–40
54. + 8:34–9:1	+ 9:23–27	80. – 12:28–34	–
55. + 9:2–10	+ 9:28–36	81. + 12:35–37a	+ 20:41–44
56. + 9:11–13	–	82. + 12:37b–40	+ 20:45–47
57. + 9:14–29	+ 9:37–43a	83. + 12:41–44	+ 21:1–4
58. + 9:30–32	+ 9:43b–45	84. + 13:1–2	+ 21:5–6
59. + 9:33–37	+ 9:46–48	85. + 13:3–8	+ 21:7–11
60. + 9:38–41	+ 9:49–50	86. + 13:9–13	+ 21:12–19
61. – 9:42–50	– X and/or C and/or ULk 9:51–18:14 (64 Lucan pericopes)	87. + 13:14–20	+ 21:20–24
		88. – 13:21–23	–
		89. +13:24–27	+ 21:25–28
62. – 10: 1	–	90. + 13:28–32	+ 21:29–33
63. – 10:2–12	–	91. – 13:33–37	– ULk 21:34–38 (2 Lucan pericopes)
64. + 10:13–16	+ 18:15–17		
65. + 10:17–22	+ 18:18–23	92. + 14:1–2	+ 22:1–2
66. + 10:23–31	+ 18:24–30	93. – 14:3–9	–
67. + 10:32–34	+ 18:31–34	94. + 14:10–11	+ 22:3–6
68. – 10:35–45	–	95. + 14:12–17	+ 22:7–14
69. + 10:46–52	+ 18:35–43 ULk 19:1–27 (2 Lucan pericopes)	96. – 14:18–21	–
70. + 11:1–10	+ 19:28–40 ULk 19:41–44 (1 Lucan pericope)	97. + 14:22–25	+ 22:15–20 X 22:21–30 (2 Lucan pericopes)
71. – 11:11	–	98. + 14:26–31	+ 22:31–34 ULk 22:35–38 (1 Lucan pericope)
72. – 11:12–14	–		
73. + 11:15–17	+ 19:45–46	99. + 14:32–42	+ 22:39–46
74. + 11:18–19	+ 19:47–48	100. + 14:43–52	+ 22:47–53
75. – 11:20–26	–	101. + 14:53–65	+ 22:54–71
		102. – 14:66–72	–

Sequence of pericopes in Mark, according to Aland's *Synopsis*	Lucan pericopes according to Aland's *Synopsis*	Sequence of pericopes in Mark, according to Aland's *Synopsis*	Lucan pericopes according to Aland's *Synopsis*
103. + 15:1	+ 23:1	109. + 15:22–26	+ 23:33–34
104. + 15:2–5	+ 23:2–5 ULk 23:6–16 (2 Lucan pericopes)	110. + 15:27–32a	+ 23:35–38
		111. + 15:32b	+ 23:39–43
105. + 15:6–14	+ 23:17–23	112. + 15:33–39	+ 23:44–48
106. + 15:15	+ 23:24–25	113. + 15:40–41	+ 23: 49
107. – 15:16–20a	–	114. + 15:42–47	+ 23:50–56
108. + 15:20b–21	+ 23:26–32	115. + 16:1–8	+ 24:1–12

question of literary dependence. And that agreement turns out to be rather insignificant: Only thirty-seven sections appear in the same sequence among ninety-one sections (40.66 percent) not dealing with the passion and resurrection. In other words, when we set aside the narratives that would be expected to follow a similar sequence, not even one-half of the sections in Mark follow the sequence of the other Synoptics.

Nevertheless, we should not overlook the fact that similarities in narrative sequence between Mark and Matthew and between Mark and Luke are considerably greater than the similarities of all three Synoptics together.

Commonalities in Matthew and Mark

In addition to the fifty-eight mentioned above, Matthew has twenty-nine other sections in common with Mark, or a total of eighty-seven of 115 (75.65 percent). Of these eighty-seven, twenty-four are passion and resurrection accounts, where the narrative order of Matthew corresponds 100 percent to that of Mark. When the remaining sixty-three sections are compared to the ninety-one total, Matthew has a 69.23 percent rate of similarity to Mark.

In general terms this means that, apart from the passion and resurrection accounts, *Matthew and Mark follow the same sequence about two-thirds of the time. If one includes those accounts, this rate of similarity rises to about three-fourths.*

Yet these figures are based on the material common to both Gospels, calculated from the standpoint of Mark. If one calculates from the standpoint of the entire scope of Matthew, a somewhat different set of percentages occurs.

In Matthew twenty-nine units cover the passion and resurrection. Since all of Mark's twenty-four sections follow the same sequence, that makes a correlation of twenty-four to twenty-nine, or 82.76 percent. Not including the passion and resurrection accounts, the sixty-three sections which correspond compare with 149 units total in Matthew, or 42.28 percent. Taking everything together, the sequence of eighty-seven Marcan sections is comparable to the order found in Matthew, which contains 178 sections. That is 48.88 percent.

In sum, for the entire Gospel of Matthew, the common narrative sequence—according to the actual count of sections—is less than half.

Commonalities in Mark and Luke

Luke shares with Mark, in addition to the fifty-eight sections mentioned above, twenty-three additional units in the same order. That is a total of eighty-one, or 70.43 percent of Mark's 115. Of these eighty-one, twenty-one are in the passion and resurrection sequence, in which Luke's rate of agreement with Mark's narrative order is 87.5 percent. The remaining sixty units comprise 65.93 percent of Mark's narrative sequence, not including the passion and resurrection accounts, or scarcely two-thirds. If one figures, not on the basis of Luke's common material with Mark, but on the basis of Luke's entire Gospel with its 186 units, then the similarities within the passion and resurrection accounts come to twenty-one out of twenty-eight or 75 percent. Apart from the passion and resurrection accounts they amount to 60 out of 158 or 37.97 percent. Comparing all of Luke to all of Mark, one arrives at eighty-one sections out of 186, or 43.55 percent.

Literary or Historical Sequence?

As a thorough investigation has shown, similarities with Mark's narrative order, when compared closely to Matthew and Luke are, then, by no means 100 percent, as one might assume in view of the oft-repeated bold assertion that "the basis for the narrative sequence in Matthew and Luke is the narrative sequence found in Mark."[6] It is not 90 percent or even 80 percent. It is barely 76 percent (Matthew) and 70 percent (Luke). Anyone who champions the view that Matthew and Luke used Mark's narrative thread as their basis must answer the questions: why did the original authors not follow Mark's account in between 25 percent and 30 percent of the sections of the original narrative order? Is it possible to maintain that Mark furnished the framework for Matthew and Luke when in Matthew the sections reflecting common narrative sequence with Mark amount to only 48.88 percent, in Luke only 43.55 percent?

In Matthew, the common narrative sequence is interrupted at one point by seven chapters (Matthew 5–11). These chapters contain 60 units. In all, 10 chapters in Matthew (1, 2, 5, 6, 7, 8, 9, 10, 11, and 25) contain no parallel to Mark's Gospel. The common narrative sequence is interrupted in numerous other places as well. Interruptions occur, first, when Marcan units have no parallel in Matthew, or no parallel in *akoluthia*; they amount to one unit nine times, two units once, three units once, five units once, six units twice, and eight units once. The sequence also does not follow when Matthew parts with Mark's narrative order for sections having no parallel in Mark, or having no parallel with Mark in *akoluthia*. This second type of divergence involves one section seven times, two sections once, and four sections once. In two cases the common sequence with Mark is interrupted by five additional sections, in one case by twenty-seven and in another by twenty-nine sections.

So what about those that are in the same order? The sections occurring in Matthew in the same order as Mark outside the passion and resurrection accounts are isolated individual sections in nine cases, a group of two sections in four cases, and a group of three sections in one case. Once four sections follow Marcan sequence, and four times five sections do. In one case we find an instance of six sections and in two cases seven sections in the same sequence without interruption. There can be no talk, therefore, of a consistent, ubiquitous "Marcan thread" by which Matthew arranges his material. Rather smaller blocks emerge, con-

6. William Wrede, *Das Messiasgeheimnis in den Evangelien*, 2d ed. (1913), 145, cited in Stoldt, *History and Criticism*, 136.

taining accounts that belong together—blocks that would stand naturally in a certain order without external pressure from another source.

The common narrative order with Mark is interrupted by Luke in no fewer than eight chapters (10, 11, 12, 13, 14, 15, 16, 17), not counting a few units out of the preceding and following chapters. In all, ten of Luke's chapters show no correspondence to Mark's narrative order (not counting the previously mentioned Luke 1 and 2).

Also in Luke, the common narrative order with Mark is often interrupted when Marcan units either have no parallels in Luke, or only a parallel that is not in the same narrative order. These interruptions, outside the passion and resurrection accounts, amount to one unit in ten cases and two units in two cases. Interruptions of four units occur twice, and in one instance we find an interruption of nine units in the common narrative order.

Luke's common narrative order with Mark is also interrupted when Luke contains units that have no Marcan parallels, or parallels that are not in *akoluthia*. Such interruptions consist of one unit in five cases and two units in three cases. There is also one block of 13 units, as well as the already mentioned block of eight chapters, encompassing 64 units.

The sections of Luke and Mark (outside the passion and resurrection accounts) that share common narrative order are isolated individual sections in five cases; four times they consist of a group of two sections and twice they consist of a group of three sections. In five instances blocks of four sections occur together. Blocks of six, seven, and eight sections occur one time each.

Summary

Without question there are similarities in the narrative order of the three synoptics; but they are not as extensive as commonly supposed. Does this *akoluthia* furnish proof that literary dependence exists between Matthew, Mark, and Luke? By no means, for the similarities may rather have a historical explanation. That becomes especially clear in the passion narrative, but it cannot be ruled out for the other parts of the gospels.

Under the presupposition that the gospels—in keeping with what they claim for themselves—relate what Jesus said and did, one would expect extensive agreement in narrative sequence. It would rather be the differences that would present a problem—but only so long as one failed to consider the possibility of each gospel's independence, or the fact that Jesus, during some three years of public activity, repeated much of what he said many times and accomplished healings of the same afflictions more than once. Under the assumption of literary dependence one must attempt to trace variations back to the original literary form. This problem falls away if the agreement between the three synoptics is historically transmitted.

Finally, it must be stated that similarities in narrative order are as murky an index for literary dependence as are agreements in content. These phenomena do not prove literary dependence; only after the probability of literary dependence is shown on more conclusive grounds can their origin be traced back to literary dependence. Anyone who lays claim to the phenomena of identical content and similarity in narrative order as "proofs" of literary dependence among the three Synoptics denies at the outset the possibility that the gospels—in keeping with what they claim for themselves—transmit what Jesus said and did. Such a claim, however, would replace scientific rigor with prejudice.

5

The Extent of Parallelism Between Matthew, Mark, and Luke

A Longitudinal Investigation

In historical-critical theology one often encounters the general claim that the entire extent of Mark's Gospel appears in Matthew and Luke (not counting, of course, the material that is unique to Mark).

Marcan Pericopes Lacking Parallel

The following sections are reckoned to be the material unique to Mark: 3:20–21, 4:26–29, 7:33–37, 8:22–26. One should, however, add 13:33–37 to this, for although this pericope does contain verses linguistically reminiscent of thematically similar pericopes in Matthew and Luke, it is not really parallel. Accordingly, both Matthew and Luke lack five Marcan pericopes, which contain a total of 347 words and comprise 3.09 percent of the entirety of Mark (see Fig. 5.1).

The pericopes of material unique to Mark are not, however, the only ones without correspondence in Matthew and Luke. There is a sizable number of pericopes that Matthew lacks, and even more that do not appear in Luke. Not including the material unique to Mark, Matthew lacks eight sections found in Mark.

Figure 5.1
Material Unique to Mark

3:20–21 = 28 words
4:26–30 = 60
7:31–37 = 114
8:22–26 = 80
13:33–37 = 65

**Total: 347 words
(3.09 percent of Mark)**

Figure 5.2
Pericopes in Mark without Parallel in Matthew

1:21–22 =31 words
1:23–28 = 92
1:35–38 = 48
3:7–12 = 102
6:30–31 = 42
9:38–40 = 55
11:18–19 = 32
12:41–44 = 75

**Total: 477 words
(4.25 percent of Mark)**

Figure 5.3

Pericopes in Mark without Parallel in Luke

1:16–20 = 82 words	9:11–13 = 52
3:28–30 = 43	10:2–10 = 97
4:32–34 = 25	10:35–40 = 112
6:1–6 = 126	11:12–14 = 55
6:18–29 = 224	11:20–26 = 101
6:45–52 = 139	14:3–9 = 125
6:53–56 = 73	14:55–61 = 89
7:1–23 = 358	15:16–20 = 63
7:24–30 = 130	**Total: 2154 words (19.18 percent of Mark)**
8:1–10 = 146	
8:14–21 = 114	

These eight contain 477 words, 4.25 percent of Mark (see Fig. 5.2). In all, therefore, Matthew lacks thirteen Marcan pericopes with 824 words, or 7.34 percent of Mark.

Luke's lack of Marcan material is considerably greater. Apart from the material unique to Mark, Luke lacks 19 Marcan pericopes[1] containing a total of 2154 words, or 19.18 percent of Mark (see Fig. 5.3). That makes no fewer than twenty-four pericopes and 22.27 percent of the entirety of Mark. Luke lacks, therefore, more than one-fifth of the content of Mark's Gospel. Insisting that Mark was a source for Luke, then, forces one to assume that Luke arbitrarily suppressed almost a fourth of the pericopes he read in Mark!

Mark's Additional Minor Details

Matthew and Luke, however, lack not only complete pericopes they allegedly read in Mark in so far as they used it as a source; they also lack much Marcan material within parallel pericopes. This material ranges in length from three words to three sentences. H. H. Stoldt has already called attention to this phenomenon, the additional minor details of Mark in comparison to Matthew and Luke.[2] He ascertained that in 180 cases the linguistic form of verses in Mark extends beyond the compass of the verses in both parallels. That would not be possible if Matthew and Luke, independently of each other, had used Mark as a source. For it strains credulity beyond the breaking point to suppose that 180 times they both—independently of each other— left out a formulation found in Mark's Gospel, formulations ranging in length from three words to three sentences. Stated quantitatively, the additional minor details of Mark listed by

1. Despite the similar sounding words about fishers of men, Luke 5:1–11 is not a parallel to Mark 1:16–20.

Luke 4:16–30 is, in spite of a few points of contact, not the same sermon in Nazareth that is reported in Mark 6:1–6a. A glance at a synopsis will easily show this, for that which Mark reports is not found in Luke, while that which Luke reports is lacking in both Mark and Matthew.

Mark 14:3-9 and Luke 7:36–50 are not parallels, for they contain no common details. They have in common only the fact that a woman comes to Jesus and anoints him.

2. H. H. Stoldt, *History and Criticism of the Marcan Hypothesis* (Dillsboro, N.C.: Western North Carolina Press, 1976), 11–17.

Stoldt run to 1498 words, or 13.43 percent of the entirety of Mark's Gospel.

Yet Stoldt's list of 180 cases is incomplete. In my study I counted seventy-eight more additional minor details, encompassing another 515 words (see Fig. 5.4). Additions consisting of one or two words were not counted, nor were ideas that Mark describes using several words where Matthew and Luke use just one

Figure 5.4

Additional Minor Details

The minor additional details found in Mark and lacking in Matthew and Luke (in addition to the 180 passages cited by Hans-Herbert Stoldt).

1:4b = 5 words	6:22b = 17	9:6b = 3	12:29 = 12
1:15a = 4[+]	6:34 = 12	9:12b = 5	12:35 = 10
1:39 = 4	6:50a = 6	9:20b = 6	13:3 = 3[+]
2:8 = 3	6:56a = 18	9:22b = 12	13:9 = 4
3:23b = 5	7:5 = 6	9:23–24 = 24	14:3 = 3
3:24b = 6	7:9 = 13	9:25a = 7	14:4 = 6
3:28b = 3	7:17 = 5	9:30b = 5	14:16a = 6
3:29b = 5	7:22 = 8	9:38 = 4	14:18b = 4
3:32a = 5	7:27a = 5	9:45 = 26	14:20 = 3
3:32b = 4	7:28b = 3	10:1 = 5	14:35b = 9
4:11 = 3	7:29b = 12	10:30b = 14	14:43b = 3
4:24 = 3	7:30a = 12	10:32b = 4[+]	14:51–52 = 19
4:38b = 6	8:1a = 13	10:46 = 4[+]	14:53b = 4
5:39a = 4	8:6b = 3	10:47 = 3	14:61a = 4
5:40a = 12	8:19b = 3	10:50 = 4[+]	15:4 = 3
6:1b = 6	8:20, 21 = 5	11:10b = 8	15:16 = 3
6:2b = 6	8:27a = 4[+]	11:13a = 5[+]	15:24 = 2[+]
6:4b = 5	8:33 = 6	11:313b = 8	16:7 = 3
6:9a = 3	8:34a = 5	11:27 = 5	10:36 = 3
6:11b = 3	8:38b = 8	**Total: 78 additional details (515 words)**	

+ More words than counted than by Stoldt, *History and Criticism of the Marcan Hypothesis* (Macon, Ga.: Mercer University Press), 1980.

Figure 5.5.   Mark's Additional Minor Details
Not Found in Matthew and Luke

Cited by Stoldt: 180 additional minor details (a total of 1498 words)

In addition: 78 additional minor details (a total of 515 words)

Total: 258 additional minor details (a total of 2013 words)

word. In all, that makes 258 additional minor details in Mark beyond the formulations of Matthew and Luke. These additions comprise 2013 words, or 17.93 percent of Mark (see Fig. 5.5). And it is probable that even this is an incomplete listing of all the additional details that closer study might turn up.

If one wishes to recognize how much of Mark is found neither in Matthew nor in Luke, one must add the material unique to Mark to the amount of Mark additional minor details. This general lack of parallelism comes to 2360 words, or 21.02 percent of the entirety of Mark's Gospel. More than a fifth of Mark's material, therefore, can be found in neither Matthew nor in Luke. This is the heavy burden that every theory of literary dependence must bear.

Proponents of such theories can follow two lines of reasoning. First, if they assume Marcan priority, they must explain how it is that Matthew and Luke, independent of each other, omitted the same pericope in their Marcan source in five separate cases. They must also explain how—independent of each other—Matthew and Luke omitted groups of words or even entire verses that were present in the Marcan exemplar in 258 cases. Second, if they assume Mark wrote after Matthew and Luke, they must explain why Mark not only added five pericopes, but also enlarged on his sources (Matthew and Luke) through his own formulations in 258 instances, although he allegedly wanted to produce a condensation of Matthew and Luke.

Yet one must go beyond even the 258 additional minor details found only in Mark. Considerable more minor details must be counted when Mark is compared to Matthew or to Luke alone. Mark has seventy-four additional minor details in comparison to Matthew alone; these additions amount to 902 words or 8.03 percent of the extent of Mark's Gospel. Added to the 258 minor details already counted, the difference in formulation between Matthew and Mark in the pericopes they have in common totals 332 additional minor details, consisting of 2915 words or 25.96 percent of Mark.

Compared to Luke, Mark adds 96 minor details, encompassing 1330 words or 11.84 percent of the Gospel. Added to the 258 additional minor details, the difference between Mark and Luke comes to 354 additional minor details, consisting of a total of 3343 words or 29.77 percent of the Marcan content.

Significance of Additional Minor Details

Based on additional minor details alone, between 26 percent and 30 percent of the formulations in Mark's text vary from parallel pericopes in the other two Synoptics. Proponents of the two-source theory are, accordingly, required to assume that Matthew crossed out around 26 percent and Luke around 30 percent of the material in their Marcan exemplar. Proponents of the Griesbach hypothesis (see p. 27) are required to assume that Mark revised some 56 percent of the words that he allegedly had before him in the sources he used!

But even that does not tell the whole story: Additional minor details also appear in Matthew and Luke in parallel pericopes. Matthew contains no fewer than 165 additional minor details not found in Mark, a total of 2270 words or 20.21 percent of the word count for Mark. Luke contains ninety-eight additional minor details that go beyond Mark's formulations in the pericopes he has in common with Mark, a total of 1324 words or 11.79 percent deviation from the word count of Mark's Gospel (see Fig. 5.6).[3]

It should be noted that the additional minor details amount to nothing less than supplementary content. Of the 165 additional minor details in Matthew, for example, we find six Old Testament prophecies (dubbed "reflective citations" in historical-critical theology). Fifteen of the additional minor details contain additional sayings of Jesus, and ninety-eight (most of them) provide additional information. Forty-six might be seen as en-

---

3. [Here and in some succeeding percentages, Linnemann is establishing the *extent of deviation* from Mark. While we cannot, strictly speaking, compare words Mark does not contain as a percentage of Mark's content, they can be measured as a deviation from a hypothetical Mark that would be in total agreement. She explains that this part of her study measures the *amount of parallelism* among Matthew, Mark, and Luke. One of the three must be used as a scale of comparison, and she has chosen to use Mark, in line with the two-source theory. "We can only measure how much Matthew must have added to Mark on the basis of the Marcan pericopes," Linnemann explains.]

Figure 5.6.   Summary, Additional Minor Details

In Mark but not Matthew: 902 words (8.03 percent of Marcan wordcount)

In Matthew but not Mark: 2270 words (20.21 percent of Marcan wordcount)

In Mark but not Luke: 1330 words (11.84 percent of Marcan wordcount)

In Luke but not Matthew: 1324 words (11.79 percent of Marcan wordcount)

largements, since what they contain is present in Mark in shorter form—but only if we have secure evidence that Matthew used Mark as a source. Defining those additional details as enlargements does not in itself prove the point, for differences must not necessarily be looked on as changes, since independent writers always differ in details.

The Case Against Literary Dependence

Mark and Matthew

One finds, as we have seen, a wide-ranging lack of parallelism between what Mark contains, on the one hand, and what Matthew and Luke contain, on the other. *The overall lack of parallelism between the three Synoptics encompasses 2360 words, or 21.02 percent of Mark.*

In the case of Matthew this lack of parallelism can be summarized:

1. Eight Marcan pericopes have no parallel in Matthew alone: 477 words (4.25 percent of Mark).
2. Seventy-four additional minor details in Mark are not in Matthew alone: 902 words (8.03 percent of Mark).
3. Matthew contains 165 additional minor details not found in Mark: 2270 words (20.21 percent deviation from Mark).
4. The total lack of parallelism between Matthew and Mark: 6009 words (53.51 percent of Mark). *This means the parallelism between Matthew and Mark is limited to 5220 words* (a 46.49 percent deviation from Mark).

Mark and Luke

The lack of parallelism between Mark and Luke alone (keeping in mind that the overall lack of parallelism among the Synoptics encompasses 2360 words or 21.02 percent of Mark) can be summarized:

1. Nineteen Marcan pericopes have no parallel in Luke alone: 2154 words (19.18 percent of Mark).
2. Ninety-six additional minor details in Mark are not in Luke alone: 1330 words (11.84 percent of Mark).
3. Ninety-eight additional minor details in Luke are not found in Mark: 1324 words (equal to a 11.79 percent deviation from Mark).
4. The total lack of parallelism between Luke and Mark: 7168 words (a portion that would be equal to 63.83 percent of Mark). This means that the parallelism between Luke and Mark is limited to just 4061 words (36.17 percent deviation from Mark).

Mark as a Source for Matthew

If one assumes that Matthew used Mark as a source, then the data call for the following scenario:

1. Matthew omitted, without replacement, from the Marcan exemplar before him, thirteen pericopes containing 824 words (7.34 percent of Mark's Gospel). On the other hand, he added a great deal of material to this source, tending not to abbreviate but rather to enlarge the exemplar.
2. Matthew abbreviated the pericopes that he used from his Marcan exemplar by some 2915 words (25.96 percent of Mark).
3. Yet Matthew enlarged those same pericopes by 2270 words (an addition representing a 20.21 percent deviation from Mark).

If Matthew used Mark as a source, the statistics show that he must have altered, by adding to or deleting from the Marcan exemplar in the pericopes from which he borrowed, by a word content equal to 49.83 percent of the book of Mark. Here is how we reach this conclusion. First we will assume that Matthew chose those sections of Mark he wished to use and discarded others. Therefore we will take the total number of words found in parallel pericopes (11,229 words) and subtract from that the total number of words found in Marcan pericopes that were omitted by Matthew (824 words; see point 1 above):

11,229 – 824 = 10,405 base words used from Mark

Second, we will add together the number of words altered through abbreviating (2915 words; see point 2 above) and enlarging (2270 words; see point 3 above):

2915 + 2270 = 5185 deviation from base words

Therefore, the level of change is the ratio of 5185 words to 10,405 words, or 49.83 percent. That does not even include changes in wording and grammatical construction! Who has the nerve to cast aspersions on Matthew the Evangelist through the unnecessary and unjustified assertion of literary dependence among the Synoptics?

Mark as a Source for Luke

If one assumes that Luke used Mark as a source, the data require maintaining that:

1. Luke omitted 24 pericopes containing 2501 words (22.27 percent of Mark) from the Marcan exemplar he used, although he added nearly twice as much material to this source, tending therefore in no sense to abbreviate but rather to enlarge the Marcan source.
2. Luke shortened the pericopes from which he borrowed by 3343 words (29.77 percent of Mark).
3. At the same time Luke enlarged those same pericopes by 1330 words (an addition equal to 11.84 percent of Mark).

If Luke used Mark as a source, the statistics show that he must have altered by addition or deletion the Marcan exemplar in the pericopes from which he borrowed a word content equal to 53.54 percent. Going through the same exercise as with Matthew, we take the total number of words found in Mark's parallel pericopes (11,229) and subtract the total number of words found in Marcan pericopes omitted by Luke (2501):

11,229 – 2501 = 8728 base words used from Mark

Adding the words used to abbreviate and enlarge gives a sum of 4673 words:

3343 + 1330 = 4673 deviation from base words

The level then of Luke's change from Mark would be the ratio of 4673 to 8728 or 53.54 percent, not including minor changes in wording and grammar! In view of these data, who wishes to risk maintaining a theory of literary dependence among the Synoptic gospels?

Summary

The Gospels are not works of literature that creatively reshape already finished material after the manner in which Goethe reshaped the popular book about Dr. Faust. The expressly stated intention of Luke is that he composed "an account of the things that have been fulfilled among us" (Luke 1:1), and that intention may be inferred to apply to the other Gospel writers as well. The burden of proof definitely falls upon the critic who would call those intentions into question.

The assumption of literary dependence among the three Synoptics, therefore, leads, in view of the data established above, to unacceptable implausibilities, indeed to absurdities. Such divergencies in the common material of the three Synoptics, if they are literally dependent, would make the evangelists into insufferable faultfinders to whom hardly a word of their source was acceptable. No evidence supports such a view, however. The great extent of similarity in content, and particularly the roughly 80 percent agreement in recording the words of Jesus, most readily shows that the writers strove for precise reporting. Also, the sort of critical excessiveness that would have to be assumed with the acceptance of literary dependence could never have resulted in the harmonious and self-consistent entities that one finds Matthew and Luke to be.

To put it succinctly: *Investigation of the extent of parallelism between Matthew, Mark, and Luke shows clearly that the data in the gospels yield no evidence for the acceptance of literary dependence among the three Synoptics. Such dependence would rather lead to absurd conclusions.*

Figures 5.7 and 5.8 summarize major findings of this section.

Figure 5.7

The Extent of Parallelism among Matthew, Mark, and Luke

Material unique to Mark:	347 words (3.09 percent of Mark)
Additional minor details in Mark not found in Matthew and Luke:	2013 words (17.93 percent of Mark)

Therefore:
The general lack of parallelism among the Synoptics encompasses 2360 words (21.02 percent of the Marcan wordcount).

Pericopes in Mark without parallel in Matthew:	477 words (4.25 percent of Mark)
Mark's additional minor details not found in Matthew:	902 words (8.43 percent of Mark)
Matthew's additional minor details not found in Mark:	2270 words (20.21 percent of Marcan wordcount)
General lack of parallels among the Synoptic Gospels:	2360 words (21.02 percent of Marcan wordcount)

Therefore:
The lack of parallelism between Matthew and Mark encompasses 6009 words (53.51 percent of the Marcan wordcount).
The extent of parallelism between Matthew and Mark encompasses 5220 words (46.49 percent of the Marcan wordcount).

Pericopes in Mark without parallel in Luke:	2154 words (19.18 percent of Mark)
Mark's additional minor details not found in Luke:	1330 words (11.84 percent of Mark)
Luke's additional minor details not found in Mark:	1324 words (11.79 percent of Marcan wordcount)
General lack of parallels among the Synoptic Gospels:	2360 words (21.02 percent of Marcan wordcount)

Therefore:
The lack of parallelism between Luke and Mark encompasses 7168 words (63.83 percent of the Marcan wordcount). The extent of parallelism between Luke and Mark encompasses 4061 words (36.17 percent of the Marcan wordcount).

Figure 5.8.   The Extent of Parallelism with Mark in Relation to the Whole of Mark's Gospel

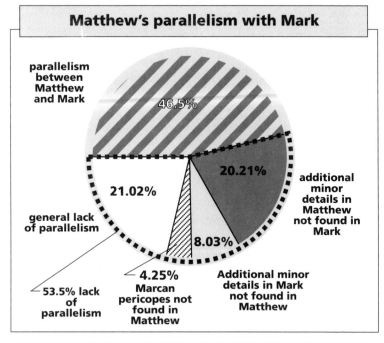

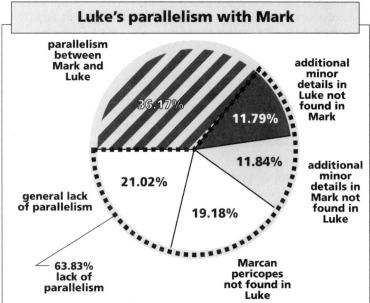

6

Quantitative Synoptic Comparison

A Representative Cross-Section

In comparing parallel Synoptic passages, historical-critical theology's presupposition of literary dependence makes allowance for a certain assumption from the outset. Just as in a well-known psychological experiment in which the person being tested focuses either on the figure of a picture or on the picture's background, exegetes generally see more or less what supports the hypothesis that they were handed before they begin their observation. The similarities in the way parallel verses are formulated are generally overemphasized. Even in the exceptional case when a scholar records both the similarities and the differences, an explanation for the differences has already been furnished by the hypothesis being championed.

Actually, given the assumption of literary dependence, one would expect similarities of nearly 100 percent. In reality that is a far cry from what one finds. Nevertheless, this unexpected lack of similarity, which places the accepted theory in question, is minimized or explained away in various ways. For example, the different words used by Matthew and Luke to replace Mark's words are said to have the same content—although that by no means speaks in favor of a literary relationship. In the same manner, differences are explained as improvements, while divergences in form (gender, tense, case, number) are minimized without taking note of the fact that the decision by Matthew or Luke to select, for example, a different tense, would have meant a weighty tampering with the exemplar. In this case Matthew and Luke did not, in fact, borrow from Mark but altered it in thoroughgoing manner. That is far more grave a matter than the mere exchange of words.

Other matters are likewise swept under the rug when they do not go along with the theory of literary dependence. For example, the omission of a whole or half sentence from Mark is dismissed with such explanations as "Matthew compresses" or "Luke shortens." On the other hand, when Matthew or Luke add a half verse, or even two or three verses, the Evangelist is "expanding," "clarifying," or "commenting." As we have established, such generalizing verdicts amount to circular reasoning: The assumption of literary dependence is used to establish it.

Such a procedure falls far short of the objectivity that one has a right to expect from scientific work. It presupposes the very thing that remains to be proven: that a literary relationship obtains among the three Synoptic Gospels, or rather, that the data found in the Synoptic Gospels make the presence of such a relationship probable.

It is, therefore, time to investigate thoroughly the data in the Synoptics, independent of any prejudgments regarding their literary interrelationships, in order to determine whether literary dependence among them is demonstrably in evidence. The extent of the similarities, as well as the differences, must be noted carefully. And this must take place, not at the (general) level of content, but at the (precise) level of linguistic form, for this alone will show whether a *literary* relationship exists. In order to arrive at usable results, the investigation must expressly avoid equating general agreement in content with identity in linguistic form; the two are by no means the same.

Analytical Method

We only can assess the data objectively through quantitative means. The sort of quantification usually done compares verses and is insufficient for our purposes. Showing similarities among verses only discloses general agreements in content. To arrive at precise results at the level of linguistic formation, it is necessary to proceed from the foundational insight that the word is the smallest significant unity. Dependence is established in comparable passages by the occurrence of words in identical form. Not only the root of the word but also its specific form in the case at hand must be scrutinized. Similarities related simply to a common root have no relevance for the question of literary dependence, since the similarity of common root is offset by the dissimilarity of divergent form.

It goes without saying that the Greek text forms the basis for quantitative analysis; as mentioned earlier, I use Kurt Aland's *Synopsis Quattuor Evangeliorum.*[1] I accept his text-critical decisions as they stand so as not to burden our task of investigating synoptic relationships with additional problems. Words in parallel verses will be regarded as identical when they agree in gender, tense, case, and number.

The investigation of the data will, then, occur through quantitative synoptic comparison. Such comparison will establish the extent of agreement among the three Synoptic Gospels within a given pericope. In order to examine the data carefully, both the similarities and the differences will be quantified.

Since the two-source theory, which assumes Marcan priority, dominates Western theology, the starting point will be the Marcan version of the pericopes examined. We will take from Aland the division of pericopes. Using the two-source theory as our point of comparison is merely a practical decision; the same methodological starting point could be carried out just as readily by using the Griesbach hypothesis.

The quantitative Synoptic comparison will proceed in four analytic steps:

1. (Stuttgart: Deutsche Bibelstiftung, 1965). [In the examples that follow Linnemann uses the 1965 edition. Newer editions, including English versions of Aland's *Synopsis of the Four Gospels,* are slightly revised. Readers checking the author's findings may come to slightly differing word counts at some points (for example, Matt. 3:13–17) or may observe different constructions than are noted in the charts below.]

Parallel Word Agreement

First, the agreements in the parallel verses of the pericope selected will be shown. This will help avoid the danger of leaving out a word. Words in parallel verses that are totally identical in all three Synoptics are depicted by blocks with heavy diagonal lines. Words that are totally identical in Matthew and Mark are shown as grey blocks. Words that are totally identical in Mark and Luke are depicted as blocks with light diagonal lines. Words that are totally identical in Matthew and Luke are represented by blocks with vertical lines. Mark's words that have no parallel are shown as solid white blocks.

"Totally identical" means words in parallel verses that agree in gender, case, number, and tense. Totally identical words also are included if they occur in a different context because of the way they transmit their content or because of their placement in the sentence. Direct parallels may transcend the boundaries of verse divisions; when parallelism in wording can be noticed, verse divisions in the respective Gospels are unimportant. Verses similar in content and form that stand within the parallel pericope at another location, are not taken into account. In these cases the difference in narrative order overrides the common formulation; it cannot contribute evidence of literary dependence. An example of how this first step of analysis is carried out may be seen in Figure 6.1.

Number of Words in Mark

Second, we determine the number of words found in the Marcan pericope. This number forms the basis (100 percent) for subsequent calculations regarding the parallel pericopes in Matthew and Luke.

Number of Identical Words

Third, we determine and count up the words found to be totally identical in the same pericope in the parallel verses. We record:

1. totally identical words in Matthew, Mark, and Luke;
2. additional identical words in Matthew and Mark;
3. additional identical words in Mark and Luke, and
4. additional identical words in Matthew and Luke.

Figure 6.1. Identical Words within Parallel Pericopes

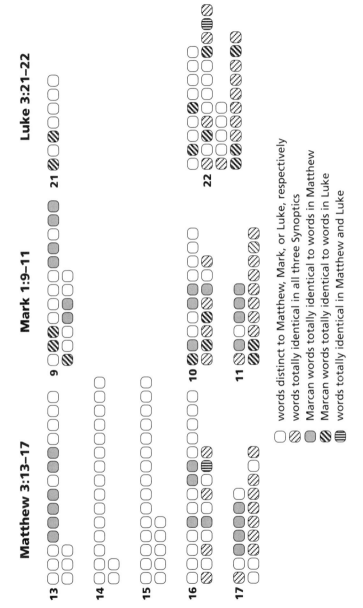

words distinct to Matthew, Mark, or Luke, respectively

words totally identical in all three Synoptics

Marcan words totally identical to words in Matthew

Marcan words totally identical to words in Luke

words totally identical in Matthew and Luke

An example of the analysis that takes place in the third step:

Mark 1:9–11: Jesus' Baptism (Marcan pericope: 53 words)

1. Totally identical words in Matthew-Mark-Luke: **12** (Note: of the 12, 7 are the words of the heavenly voice! That is 58.33 percent of the identical words.).
2. Matthew-Mark: **14** additional totally identical words (**14 + 12 = 26**).
3. Mark-Luke: **9** additional totally identical words (**9 + 12 = 21**).
4. Matthew-Luke: **1** additional totally identical word (**1 + 12 = 13**).

A total of 22.64 percent of the words used in Mark 1:9–11 are identical in both Matthew 3:13–17 and Luke 3:21–22—or less than one-fourth. Matthew and Mark agree in 49 percent of the words in the parallel verses, Mark and Luke in 39.62 percent, Matthew and Luke in 24.53 percent.

If one assumes that Matthew used Mark's Gospel, then one must argue that Matthew altered 51 percent of the words of his exemplar (100 percent minus 49 percent). If one assumes the use of Mark's Gospel by Luke, then Luke must have altered 60.38 percent of the words of the exemplar he had before him (100 percent minus 39.62 percent). Advocating literary dependence here amounts to absurdity.

It is highly improbable, to put it mildly, that Matthew and Luke either interchanged the words of their source or altered them in tense, case, gender, or number over one-half of the time. They were not, after all, freelance writers who used the Marcan text simply as the subject of their own creative production. How great their concern was for precise reportage is suggested by their agreement in the words of the heavenly voice in the pericope analyzed above: seven of the nine words are identical (77.78 percent). One can only conclude that the data in that pericope do not speak in favor of assuming literary dependence, but rather against it.

Differences among the Pericopes

In a fourth analytical step we establish the differences among Matthew, Mark, and Luke. Although the starting point of the investigation is the alleged literary dependence of the three Synoptic Gospels, the investigation cannot complete its task if observations consider the results of analysis from just one vantage point. For the differences between Matthew and Mark are not the same as those between Mark and Luke. So we must determine in separate stages where Matthew, and then Luke, differ from Mark in the parallels of the pericope in question. We will illustrate this quantitative Synoptic comparison by using the baptismal pericope of Mark 1:9–11; Matthew 3:13–17, and Luke 3:21–22 (figs. 6.2, 6.3).

In the lists comprising these figures, differences in parallel verses are numbered consecutively for Matthew in Figure 6.2 and for Luke in 6.3. They are marked with a *plus* (+) for each added word and a *minus* (–) for each missing word. A different word or a word having a different form is designated by *instead*. Different word order in parallel verses is also recorded.

Each word is listed in the same manner, whether it is a one-letter article or a substantive with five syllables, for every word adds a component in the totality that distinguishes Matthew and Luke from Mark. For purposes of linguistic investigation each word must be regarded as a unit of measure, like a gram or a second. If Matthew or Luke have a sentence with ten extra words, then every word counts individually, so the full weight of difference comes into view. If Matthew or Luke lack a sentence found at the same juncture in Mark, this difference must be counted according to the number of words in that sentence. For the difference takes its true form from the relative length of the sentences, be they longer or shorter.

The Marcan pericope contains fifty-three words; twelve of them are identical in the parallel verses of Matthew and Luke. The differences in the parallel verses add up to eighty-two words in Matthew and forty-three in Luke. Differences in Matthew and in Luke are shown in figures 6.2 and 6.3, respectively.

The differences recorded in our fourth step of analysis result from:

1. different word choice;
2. different word form (difference in gender, case, tense, or number);
3. different placement of words or sentence construction;

Figure 6.2.   Differences in the text of Matthew 3:13–17 (As Compared with Mark 1:9–11)

1. + τότε
2. – καὶ
3. – ἐγένετο
4. – ἐν
5. – ἐκείναις
6. – ταῖς
7. – ἡμέραις
8. παραγίνεται instead of ἦλθεν
9. + ὁ
10. – Ναζαρὲθ
11. + πρὸς
12. + τὸν
13. + Ἰωάννην
14. + τοῦ
15. + βαπτισθῆναι
16. + ὑπ᾽
17. + αὐτοῦ
18. + ὁ
19. + δὲ
20. + Ἰωάννης
21. + διεκώλυεν
22. + αὐτὸν
23. + λέγων
24. + ἐγὼ
25. + χρείαν
26. + ἔχω
27. + ὑπὸ
28. + σοῦ
29. + βαπτισθῆναι
30. + καὶ
31. + σὺ

32. + ἔρχῃ
33. + πρός
34. + με
35. + ἀποκριθεὶς
36. + δὲ
37. + ὁ
38. + Ἰησοῦς
39. + εἶπεν
40. + πρὸς
41. + αὐτῷ
42. + ἄφες
43. + ἄρτι
44. + οὕτως
45. + γὰρ
46. + πρέπον
47. + ἐστὶν
48. + ἡμῖν
49. + πληρῶσαι
50. + πᾶσαν
51. + δικαιοσύνην
52. + τότε
53. + ἀφίησιν
54. + αὐτόν
55. – καὶ
56. βαπτισθεὶς instead of ἐβαπτίσθη
57. + δὲ
58. + ὁ
59. + Ἰησοῦς
60. ἐπὶ instead of εἰς
61. – ὑπὸ

62. – Ἰωάννου
63. – καὶ
64. ἀνέβη instead of ἀναβαίνων
65. ἀπὸ instead of ἐκ
66. + καὶ
67. + ἰδοὺ
68. εἶδεν (connection differs)
69. ἠνεῴχθησαν instead of σχιζομένους
70. οἱ instead of τοὺς
71. οὐρανοί instead of οὐρανοὺς
72. – τὸ
73. + θεοῦ
74. ὡσεὶ instead of ὡς
75. ἐρχόμενον instead of καταβαῖνον
76. ἐπ᾽ instead of εἰς
77. + ἰδοὺ
78. – ἐγένετο
79. + λέγουσα
80. οὗτος instead of σὺ
81. ἐστιν instead of εἶ
82. ᾧ instead of σοὶ

+ additional in Matthew
– lacking in Matthew

4. different placement of verses within the pericope;
5. additional minor details in Mark not found in Matthew or Luke or both;

6. additional minor details in Matthew or Luke not found in Mark, or

7. possibly other factors.

The quantitative synoptic comparison, with its four analytic steps, furnishes a means of investigating individual pericopes to determine whether they provide evidence of literary dependence. The results of the investigation of individual pericopes are then summarized in cross-section format and assessed in order to come to a well-founded decision.

In order not to delay publication of the results, I have contented myself with a representative cross-section and subjected just thirty-five Marcan pericopes to this four-step investigation. I have taken pains to select pericopes with considerable agreement in the parallel passages, those that might be thought to best argue for literary dependence. I have chosen several peri-

Figure 6.3. Differences in the Text of Luke 3:21–22 (As Compared with Mark 1:9–11)

1. δὲ instead of καὶ	18. – εἰς	33. καταβῆναι
2. – ἐκείναις	19. – τὸν	instead of
3. – ταῖς	20. – Ἰορδάνην	καταβαῖνον
4. – ἡμέραις	21. – ὑπὸ	(also different
5. + τῷ	22. – Ἰωάννου	placement)
6. + βαπτισθῆναι	23. – εὐθὺς	34. + τὸ
7. + ἅπαντα	24. – ἀναβαίνων	35. + ἅγιον
8. + τὸν	25. – ἐκ	36. + σωματικῷ
9. + λαὸν	26. – τοῦ	37. + εἴδει
10. – ἦλθεν	27. – ὕδατος	38. ἐπ᾽ instead of εἰς
11. Ἰησοῦ instead of Ἰησοῦς	28. + προσευχομένου	39. φωνὴν instead of φωνὴ
12. – ἀπὸ	29. – εἶδεν	40. ἐξ instead of ἐκ
13. – Ναζαρὲθ	30. ἀνεῳχθῆναι instead of σχιζομένους	41. – τῶν
14. – τῆς	31. τὸν instead of τοὺς	42. οὐρανοῦ instead of οὐρανῶν
15. – Γαλιλαίας	32. οὐρανὸν instead of οὐρανοὺς	43. γενέσθαι instead of ἐγένετο
16. βαπτισθέντος instead of ἐβαπτίσθη		
17. + καὶ		

+ additional in Luke
– lacking in Luke

copes from every chapter of Mark (except chapter 16). Pericopes chosen repeatedly represent all the *Gattungen* or different literary forms postulated by form criticism. The thirty-five pericopes encompass 3911 words—34.83 percent or more than one-third of the Gospel.

The weight of this cross-sectional investigation is considerably greater than might first appear. Thirty-two Marcan pericopes with 2976 words, or 26.5 percent of Mark, are automatically exempt from such investigation because they lack parallel in Matthew or Luke. Fourteen additional pericopes (1208 words, 10.75 percent of Mark's Gospel) show so few parallels that it would make little sense to investigate them in a cross-section comparison (see figs. 6.4, 6.5).

To summarize figures 6.4 and 6.5: Due to a lack of parallels or deficient parallels, forty-six Marcan pericopes, containing a total of 4184 words or 37.26 percent of the Gospel, are *not* eligible for quantitative cross-sectional comparison.

Figure 6.4

Marcan Pericopes Lacking Parallels in Matthew or Luke or Both

1:16–20 = 82 words	6:30–31 = 42	10:2–10 = 97
1:21–22 = 31	6:45–52 = 139	10:35–40 = 112
1:23–28 = 92	6:53–56 = 73	11:12–14 = 54
1:35–38 = 48	7:1–23 = 358	11:18–19 = 32
3:7–12 = 102	7:24–30 = 130	11:20–26 = 101
3:20–21 = 28	7:31–37 = 114	12:41–44 = 75
3:28–30 = 43	8:1–10 = 146	13:33–37 = 65
4:26–29 = 60	8:14–21 = 114	14:3–9 = 124
4:33–34 = 25	8:22–26 = 80	14:55–61a = 89
6:1–6a = 126	9:11–13 = 52	15:16–20a = 63
6:18–29 = 224	9:38–40 = 55	

Total: 2976 words (26.50 percent of Mark)

Figure 6.5

Marcan Pericopes for which Parallels in Mattthew or Luke or Both Are Deficient

1:2–6 = 91 words	9:42–50 = 149	14:22–25 = 68
1:12–13 = 30	12:37b–40 = 51	14:26–31 = 87
4:21–25 = 76	13:22–23 = 36	15:6–14 = 104
8:11–13 = 47	13:24–27 = 51	15:27–32a = 72
9:14–29 = 268	14:18–21 = 78	

Total: 1208 words (10.75 percent of Mark)

In light of the above, we conclude that 7045 words, or 62.74 percent of the text of Mark's Gospel can be effectively investigated. Based on this amount, the thirty-five pericopes studied in Figure 6.6 below comprise 3911 words, or 55.51 percent of the portions of Mark with significant parallels in Matthew or Luke, somewhat more than half of all pericopes on which investigation would be meaningful.

Figure 6.6

Cross-sectional Quantitative Synoptic Investigation

All pericopes taken from the Gospel of Mark. Words in quotation marks refer to the *Gattungen* (the hypothesized literary forms or genres of form criticism).

1. **1:9–11: Jesus' Baptism** (53 words in Mark)	
"Legend"	
Identical in Matthew-Mark-Luke:	12
Identical in Matthew-Luke:	1
Identical in Matthew-Mark:	14
Identical in Mark-Luke:	9
14 + 12 = 26 words identical in Matthew-Mark, but 82 differences	
9 + 12 = 21 words identical in Mark-Luke, but 43 differences	
2. **1:29–34: Healing of Peter's Mother-in-law** (90 words)	
"Healing miracle"	
Identical in Matthew-Mark-Luke:	8

Identical in Matthew-Luke:	0
Identical in Matthew-Mark:	11
Identical in Mark-Luke:	19

11 + 8 = 19 words identical in Matthew-Mark, but 96 differences

19 + 8 = 27 words identical in Mark-Luke, but 109 differences

3. 1:40–45: Cleansing of the Leper (98 words)

"Healing miracle"

Identical in Matthew-Mark-Luke:	31
Identical in Matthew-Luke:	2
Identical in Matthew-Mark:	5
Identical in Mark-Luke:	7

5 + 31 = 36 words identical in Matthew-Mark, but 79 differences

7 + 31 = 38 words identical in Mark-Luke, but 98 differences

4. 2:1–12: Healing of the Paralytic (197 words)

"Miracle story with apophthegm"

Identical in Matthew-Mark-Luke:	52
Identical in Matthew-Luke:	8
Identical in Matthew-Mark:	21
Identical in Mark-Luke:	22

21 + 52 = 73 words identical in Matthew-Mark, but 157 differences

22 + 52 = 74 words identical in Mark-Luke, but 223 differences

5. 2:23–28: Plucking Grain on the Sabbath (108 words)

"Apophthegm"

Identical in Matthew-Mark-Luke:	39
Identical in Matthew-Luke:	2
Identical in Matthew-Mark:	11
Identical in Mark-Luke:	11

11 + 39 = 50 words identical in Matthew-Mark, but 122 differences

11 + 39 = 50 words identical in Mark-Luke, but 69 differences

6. 3:1–6: The Man with the Withered Hand (94 words)

"Healing miracle"

Identical in Matthew-Mark-Luke:	14
Identical in Matthew-Luke:	2
Identical in Matthew-Mark:	20

Identical in Mark-Luke:	22

20 + 14 = 34 words identical in Matthew-Mark, but 97 differences

22 + 14 = 36 words identical in Mark-Luke, but 103 differences

7. 3:31–35: The Mother and Brothers of Jesus (83 words)

"Biographical apophthegm"

Identical in Matthew-Mark-Luke:	19
Identical in Matthew-Luke:	5
Identical in Matthew-Mark:	26
Identical in Mark-Luke:	1

26 + 19 = 45 words identical in Matthew-Mark, but 71 differences

1 + 19 = 20 words identical in Mark-Luke, but 82 differences

8. 4:1–9: The Parable of the Sower (151 words)

Identical in Matthew-Mark-Luke:	37
Identical in Matthew-Luke:	1
Identical in Matthew-Mark:	44
Identical in Mark-Luke:	6

44 + 37 = 81 words identical in Matthew-Mark, but 91 differences

6 + 37 = 43 words identical in Mark-Luke, but 91 differences

9. 4:10–12: The Purpose of the Parable (52 words)

Identical in Matthew-Mark-Luke:	8
Identical in Matthew-Luke:	7
Identical in Matthew-Mark:	3
Identical in Mark-Luke:	10

3 + 8 = 11 words identical in Matthew-Mark, but 163 differences

10 + 8 = 18 words identical in Mark-Luke, but 42 differences

10. 4:13–20: Explanation of the Parable of the Sower (146 words)

Identical in Matthew-Mark-Luke:	16
Identical in Matthew-Luke:	1
Identical in Matthew-Mark:	36
Identical in Mark-Luke:	19

36 + 16 = 52 words identical in Matthew-Mark, but 125 differences

19 + 16 = 35 words identical in Mark-Luke, but 147 differences

11. 5:21–43: Jairus' Daughter; the Woman Who Touched Jesus' Garment (374 words)

"Healing miracle"

Identical in Matthew-Mark-Luke:	25
Identical in Matthew-Luke:	3
Identical in Matthew-Mark:	22
Identical in Mark-Luke:	65

22 + 25 = 47 words identical in Matthew-Mark, but 373 differences

65 + 25 = 90 words identical in Mark-Luke, but 392 differences

12. 6:14–16: The Death of John the Baptist (54 words)

Identical in Matthew-Mark-Luke:	5
Identical in Matthew-Luke:	3
Identical in Matthew-Mark:	8
Identical in Mark-Luke:	15

8 + 5 = 13 words identical in Matthew-Mark, but 54 differences

15 + 5 = 20 words identical in Mark-Luke, but 59 differences

13. 6:32–44: The Feeding of the Five Thousand (194 words)

"Nature miracle"

Identical in Matthew-Mark-Luke:	41
Identical in Matthew-Luke:	12
Identical in Matthew-Mark:	41
Identical in Mark-Luke:	12

41 + 41 = 82 words identical in Matthew-Mark, but 170 differences

12 + 41 = 53 words identical in Mark-Luke, but 226 differences

14. 8:27–33: Peter's Confession and Jesus' First Passion Prediction (144 words)

Identical in Matthew-Mark-Luke:	37
Identical in Matthew-Luke:	9
Identical in Matthew-Mark:	44
Identical in Mark-Luke:	11

44 + 37 = 81 words identical in Matthew-Mark, but 182 differences

11 + 37 = 48 words identical in Mark-Luke, but 111 differences

15. 8:34–9:1: Call to Discipleship (135 words)

"Logia"

Identical in Matthew-Mark-Luke:	65
Identical in Matthew-Luke:	0

Identical in Matthew-Mark: 13
Identical in Mark-Luke: 18
13 + 65 = 78 words identical in Matthew-Mark, but 83 differences
18 + 65 = 83 words identical in Mark-Luke, but 74 differences

16. 9:2–8: The Transfiguration (121 words)

"Legend"

Identical in Matthew-Mark-Luke: 41
Identical in Matthew-Luke: 8
Identical in Matthew-Mark: 32
Identical in Mark-Luke: 6
32 + 41 = 73 words identical in Matthew-Mark, but 103 differences
6 + 41 = 47 words identical in Mark-Luke, but 187 differences

17. 9:30–32: Second Passion Prediction (47 words)

Identical in Matthew-Mark-Luke: 7
Identical in Matthew-Luke: 3
Identical in Matthew-Mark: 5
Identical in Mark-Luke: 8
5 + 7 = 12 words identical in Matthew-Mark, but 39 differences
8 + 7 = 15 words identical in Mark-Luke, but 67 differences

18. 9:33–37: Who Is the Greatest? (85 words)

"Biographical apophthegm"

Identical in Matthew-Mark-Luke: 15
Identical in Matthew-Luke: 1
Identical in Matthew-Mark: 4
Identical in Mark-Luke: 11
4 + 15 = 19 words identical in Matthew-Mark, but 117 differences
11 + 15 = 26 words identical in Mark-Luke, but 89 differences

19. 10:13–16: Little Children Blessed (64 words)

"Biographical apophthegm"

Identical in Matthew-Mark-Luke: 21
Identical in Matthew-Luke: 1
Identical in Matthew-Mark: 6
Identical in Mark-Luke: 24
6 + 21 = 27 words identical in Matthew-Mark, but 48 differences

24 + 21 = 45 words identical in Mark-Luke, but 25 differences

20. **10:32–34: Jesus' Third Passion Prediction** (73 words)	
Identical in Matthew-Mark-Luke:	11
Identical in Matthew-Luke:	4
Identical in Matthew-Mark:	18
Identical in Mark-Luke:	3

18 + 11 = 29 words identical in Matthew-Mark, but 54 differences

3 + 11 = 14 words identical in Mark-Luke, but 83 differences

21. **10:46–52: The Healing of Blind Bartimaeus** (123 words)	
"Healing miracle"	
Identical in Matthew-Mark-Luke:	23
Identical in Matthew-Luke:	4
Identical in Matthew-Mark:	4
Identical in Mark-Luke:	29

4 + 23 = 27 words identical in Matthew-Mark, but 104 differences

29 + 23 = 52 words identical in Mark-Luke, but 105 differences

22. **11:1–10: The Triumphal Entry** (164 words)	
"Narrative"	
Identical in Matthew-Mark-Luke:	37
Identical in Matthew-Luke:	15
Identical in Matthew-Mark:	25
Identical in Mark-Luke:	26

25 + 37 = 62 words identical in Matthew-Mark, but 172 differences

26 + 37 = 63 words identical in Mark-Luke, but 183 differences

23. **11:15–17: Cleansing of the Temple** (65 words)	
"Narrative"	
Identical in Matthew-Mark-Luke:	18
Identical in Matthew-Luke:	0
Identical in Matthew-Mark:	20
Identical in Mark-Luke:	3

20 + 18 = 38 words identical in Matthew-Mark, but 30 differences

3 + 18 = 21 words identical in Mark-Luke, but 48 differences

24. **11:27–33: The Authority of Jesus Questioned** (125 words)	
"Apophthegm"	

Identical in Matthew-Mark-Luke:	52
Identical in Matthew-Luke:	4
Identical in Matthew-Mark:	27
Identical in Mark-Luke:	14

27 + 52 = 79 words identical in Matthew-Mark, but 63 differences

14 + 52 = 66 words identical in Mark-Luke, but 86 differences

25. 12:1–12: Parable of the Vineyard and the Tenants (181 words)

"Parable"

Identical in Matthew-Mark-Luke:	51
Identical in Matthew-Luke:	20
Identical in Matthew-Mark:	38
Identical in Mark-Luke:	29

38 + 51 = 89 words identical in Matthew-Mark, but 211 differences

29 + 51 = 80 words identical in Mark-Luke, but 148 differences

26. 12:13–17: Paying Taxes to Caesar (105 words)

"Apophthegm"

Identical in Matthew-Mark-Luke:	30
Identical in Matthew-Luke:	2
Identical in Matthew-Mark:	30
Identical in Mark-Luke:	13

30 + 30 = 60 words identical in Matthew-Mark, but 75 differences

13 + 30 = 43 words identical in Mark-Luke, but 79 differences

27. 13:1–8: Destruction of the Temple Foretold (132 words)

Identical in Matthew-Mark-Luke:	43
Identical in Matthew-Luke:	4
Identical in Matthew-Mark:	28
Identical in Mark-Luke:	7

28 + 43 = 71 words identical in Matthew-Mark, but 90 differences

7 + 43 = 50 words identical in Mark-Luke, but 114 differences

28. 13:9–13: Warning of Persecution (97 words)

Identical in Matthew-Mark-Luke:	19
Identical in Matthew-Luke:	2
Identical in Matthew-Mark:	45
Identical in Mark-Luke:	1

45 + 19 = 64 words identical in Matthew-Mark, but 69 differences
1 + 19 = 20 words identical in Mark-Luke, but 129 differences

29. **14:1–2: The Plot to Kill Jesus** (34 words)	
"Narrative"	
Identical in Matthew-Mark-Luke:	4
Identical in Matthew-Luke:	0
Identical in Matthew-Mark:	12
Identical in Mark-Luke:	5

12 + 4 = 16 words identical in Matthew-Mark, but 58 differences
5 + 4 = 9 words identical in Mark-Luke, but 31 differences

30. **Mark 14:10–11: Judas' Agreement to Betray Jesus** (30 words)	
"Narrative"	
Identical in Matthew-Mark-Luke:	5
Identical in Matthew-Luke:	1
Identical in Matthew-Mark:	6
Identical in Mark-Luke:	5

6 + 5 = 11 words identical in Matthew-Mark, but 33 differences
5 + 5 = 10 words identical in Mark-Luke, but 42 differences

31. **14:12–17: Preparation for the Passover** (111 words)	
"Legend"	
Identical in Matthew-Mark-Luke:	19
Identical in Matthew-Luke:	1
Identical in Matthew-Mark:	19
Identical in Mark-Luke:	27

19 + 19 = 38 words identical in Matthew-Mark, but 80 differences
27 + 19 = 46 words identical in Mark-Luke, but 86 differences

32. **14:42–53: The Betrayal and Arrest of Jesus** (141 words)	
"Narrative"	
Identical in Matthew-Mark-Luke:	34
Identical in Matthew-Luke:	9
Identical in Matthew-Mark:	52
Identical in Mark-Luke:	3

52 + 34 = 86 words identical in Matthew-Mark, but 138 differences
3 + 34 = 37 words identical in Mark-Luke, but 175 differences

33. 15:2–5: Jesus before Pilate (48 words)

"Narrative"	
Identical in Matthew-Mark-Luke:	11
Identical in Matthew-Luke:	1
Identical in Matthew-Mark:	12
Identical in Mark-Luke:	4

12 + 11 = 23 words identical in Matthew-Mark, but 50 differences

4 + 11 = 15 words identical in Mark-Luke, but 91 differences

34. 15:22–26: The Crucifixion (55 words)

"Narrative"	
Identical in Matthew-Mark-Luke:	7
Identical in Matthew-Luke:	2
Identical in Matthew-Mark:	14
Identical in Mark-Luke:	2

14 + 7 = 21 words identical in Matthew-Mark, but 51 differences

2 + 7 = 9 words identical in Mark-Luke, but 71 differences

35. 16:1–8: The Empty Tomb (137 words)

"Legend"	
Identical in Matthew-Mark-Luke:	10
Identical in Matthew-Luke:	0
Identical in Matthew-Mark:	19
Identical in Mark-Luke:	7

19 + 10 = 29 words identical in Matthew-Mark, but 212 differences

7 + 10 = 17 words identical in Mark-Luke, but 220 differences

Totals for parallel pericopes

Number of words in 35 pericopes:	3911
Identical in Matthew-Mark-Luke:	867
Identical in Matthew-Mark:	1603
Different in Matthew-Mark	3742
Different in Mark-Luke	3928
Identical in Mark-Luke:	1341
Identical in Matthew-Luke:	135

Graphically this can be illustrated as in Fig. 6.7.

Figure 6.7.   Quantitative Synoptic Comparison: *Result of a Representative Cross-section*

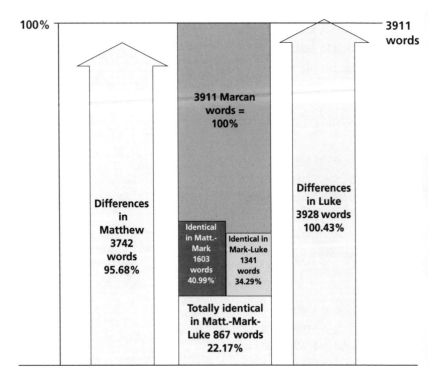

Summary

A total of 7045 words, or 62.74 percent of Mark, can be meaningfully analyzed quantitatively. The above tables cover 4184 words, or 59.39 percent of the 7045 total. These thirty-five pericopes, then, include 34.83 percent of the entire Gospel.

In the thirty-five pericopes investigated above only 867 words out of 3911 words are shared by all three Synoptics. That is not even one-fourth. And of this 22.17 percent, a considerable portion consists of Jesus' words, which by my estimate show an agreement in wording of nearly 80 percent. The 22.17 percent also includes nondescript, basic words without which sentences cannot be formulated, while other words are prescribed, given the content of the material. Such relatively trivial word-for-word agreement furnishes no evidence for literary dependence.

This holds true even if one does not insist on agreement among all three Synoptics but is rather content with similarity between just two. Between Matthew and Mark there is a total of just 1603 totally identical words in parallel verses, or 40.99 percent of the portion of Mark investigated. Mark and Luke have 1341 totally identical words in parallel verses, or 34.29 percent of the portion of Mark investigated. Matthew and Luke contain 137 identical words in parallel verses, 3.5 percent of the 3911 words.

The differences, however, between Matthew and Mark, or between Mark and Luke, go beyond just bringing the percentage figures up to 100 percent, in which case the differences would already have turned out to be considerably greater than the similarities. The numbers even show a surplus of differences, because they are not limited to just word choice and word form. The differences between Matthew and Mark come to 3742 of the 3911 words under investigation, or 95.68 percent. The differences between Luke and Mark come to 3928 of the 3911 words under investigation, or 100.43 percent words (see Fig. 6.7). In other words, for every 100 Marcan words there are 95.68 differences in Matthew and 100.43 differences in Luke.

Does this speak in favor of literary dependence?

7

The Significance
of the Extent of Similarities
in Vocabulary

We now will augment our cross–sectional investigation of chapter 6 with a longitudinal study. If the Synoptics are literarily interdependent, if they used each other as sources or were dependent on a common source, then a linguistic deposit must be evident. Similarities in vocabulary will exceed in a striking manner similarities found in other writings treating the same object, using the same language, and hailing from the same epoch. The only case in which such a linguistic deposit would not be expected is if authors used a source only as inspiration and material for their own creativity and literary invention. But that does not describe the evangelists; there are too many similarities in content and sequence of pericopes, as well as the far-reaching linguistic agreement in passages containing words of Jesus. Precisely in view of the measurable similarities in content, sequence, and form, every divergence of Matthew and Luke from Mark speaks against literary dependence.

The Level of Vocabulary Agreement

The vocabulary of Mark encompasses, according to Robert Morgenthaler, 1345 words.[1] One would expect that, if not 100 percent, then 90 percent or at least 80 percent of this vocabulary should appear in Matthew and Luke. The presupposition that Matthew and Luke used Mark as a source means every word exchange intrudes into the exemplar. One would expect this to occur only where some justified offense might be taken at the original word or where the user of the source automatically, occasionally, and unconsciously used some more familiar word as he copied. Only in the former case can one reckon with the possibility that Matthew and Luke agree on the exclusion of a certain word—but I do not suggest that such agreement must be looked on as probable.

It should, therefore, astonish every proponent of the two-source theory (or other theories of literary dependence) that no fewer than 187 words of Mark's vocabulary appear in neither Matthew nor Luke (see Fig. 7.1). That means dependent Matthew and Luke obliterated 13.5 percent of Mark's vocabulary—*and did so in full mutual agreement, but totally independent of each other!* Anyone wishing to hold to the two-source theory must swallow this unpalatable fact, whose unsavory presence must be faced by proponents of other literary dependence theories as well.

Matthew, Mark, and Luke have in common just 830 words or 61.71 percent of the vocabulary of Mark's Gospel. That is little more than three-fifths, a quite unexpected result, for extensive identity in vocabulary normally accompanies direct literary dependence. In exceptional cases one would allow for linguistic alterations by abbreviation, expansion, or attempted improvements. But it seems hardly likely that someone who thinks a piece of writing worth using as an exemplar would then turn around and criticize it sentence by sentence and word by word. Such a process only could be the mark of some notorious faultfinder. The assumption that both Matthew and Luke were cavilers of that ilk lies outside all probability.

1. Robert Morgenthaler, *Statistitik des neutestamentlichen Wortschatzes* (Zurich/Frankfurt: Gotthelf, 1958), 164.

Figure 7.1.   Words Occurring in Mark but Not in Matthew and Luke

1. ἀββά
2. Ἀβιαθάρ
3. ἀγρεύειν
4. ἀκάνθινος
5. ἀλαλάζειν
6. ἄλαλος
7. ἀλεκτοροφωνία
8. Ἀλέξανδρος
9. ἀλλαχοῦ
10. ἁμάρτημα
11. ἀμφιβάλλειν
12. ἄμφοδον
13. ἀναθεματίζειν
14. ἀνακυλίειν
15. ἀναλαμβάνειν
16. ἄναλος
17. ἀναμιμνήσκειν
18. ἀναπηδᾶν
19. ἀναστενάζειν
20. ἀποβάλλειν
21. ἀπόδημος
22. ἀποκόπτειν
23. ἀποπλανᾶν
24. ἀποστεγάζειν
25. ἀποστερεῖν
26. ἀσέλγεια
27. ἀσφαλῶς
28. αὐτόματος
29. ἀφρίζειν
30. ἀφροσύνη
31. ἀχειροποίητος
32. βαπτισμός
33. βαρτιμαῖος
34. βεβαιοῦν
35. βοανηργές
36. βροντή
37. γναφεύς
38. Δαλμανουθά
39. δαμάζειν
40. διαγίνεσθαι

41. διακόσιοι
42. διαλέγεσθαι
43. διασπᾶν
44. διαστέλλεσθαι
45. δισχίλιοι
46. δρέπανον
47. δύσκολος
48. δωρεῖσθαι
49. εἰρηνεύειν
50. εἶτεν
51. ἐκθαμβεῖσθαι
52. ἐκθαυμάζειν
53. ἐκπερισσῶς
54. ἔκφοβος
55. Ἑλληνίς
56. ἐλωί
57. ἐναγκαλίζεσθαι
58. ἐνειλεῖν
59. ἔννυχα
60. ἐνταφιασμός
61. ἐξάπινα
62. ἐξαυτῆς
63. ἐξορύσσειν
64. ἐξουδενεῖν
65. ἐπαγγέλλεσθαι
66. ἐπακολουθεῖν
67. ἐπιγράφειν
68. ἐπιλύειν
69. ἐπιράπτειν
70. ἐπίστασθαι
71. ἐπισυντρέχειν
72. ἐσμυρνισμένον
73. ἐσχάτως
74. εὐκαιρεῖν
75. εὔκαιρος
76. εὐκαίρως
77. εὐσχήμων
78. ἐφφαθά
79. ἡδέως
80. θαμβεῖν

81. θανάσιμος
82. θερμαίνεσθαι
83. θηρίον
84. θυγάτριον
85. θυρωρός
86. Ἰδουμαία
87. Ἱεροσολυμῖται
88. Ἰωσῆς
89. καταβαρύνειν
90. καταδιώκειν
91. κατακόπτειν
92. καταλαμβάνειν
93. κατατίθεναι
94. κατευλογεῖν
95. κατοίκησις
96. κεντυρίων
97. κεφαλαιοῦν
98. κοινός
99. κοῦμ
100. κράβατος
101. κτίσις
102. κυλίεσθαι
103. κύπτειν
104. κωμόπολις
105. λευκαίνειν
106. μεγιστάν
107. μηκύνηται
108. μισθωτός
109. μογιλάλος
110. μορφή
111. μυρίσαι
112. νάρδος
113. νουνεχῶς
114. ξέστης
115. ὁλοκαύτωμα
116. ὁρκίζειν
117. οὐά
118. παιδιόθεν
119. παραδέχεσθαι
120. παρόμοιος

121. παρρησία	144. ῥαντίζειν	166. Συροφοινίκισσα
122. περιτρέχειν	145. ῥάπισμα	167. σύσσημον
123. περιθέρειν	146. Ῥοῦφος	168. ταλιθά
124. πηγή	147. Σαλώμη	169. τηλαυγῶς
125. πιστικός	148. σανδάλιον	170. Τιμαῖος
126. πολυτελής	149. σκώληξ	171. τριακόσιοι
127. πρασιά	150. σμυρνίζειν	172. τρίζει
128. προαύλιον	151. σπάσθαι	173. τρόμος
129. προλαμβάνειν	152. σπεκουλάτωρ	174. τρυμαλιά
130. προμεριμνᾶτε	153. στασιαστής	175. ὑπερηφανία
131. προσάββατον	154. στενάζειν	176. ὑπερπερισσῶς
132. προσαίτης	155. στήκειν	177. ὑποδεῖσθαι
133. προσκαρτερεῖν	156. στιβάς	178. ὑπολήνιον
134. προσκεφάλειον	157. στίλβειν	179. ὑστέρησις
135. προσορμίζεσθαι	158. συγκαθήμενος	180. φανεροῦν
136. προσπορεύεσθαι	159. συλλυπεῖσθαι	181. φανερῶς
137. προστρέχειν	160. συμπόσιον	182. χαλκίον
138. πρύμνα	161. συναναβαίνειν	183. χειροποίητος
139. πτυρας	162. συναποθανεῖν	184. χιλίαρχος
140. πυγμή	163. συνεργεῖν	185. χλωρός
141. πωροῦν	164. συνθλίβειν	186. χοῦς
142. πώρωσις	165. συντρέχειν	187. ὠτάριον
143. ῥαββουνί		

But of the 830 words common to Matthew, Mark, and Luke, a large number belong to the basic word stock necessary for verbal communication: articles and pronouns, conjunctions and prepositions, auxiliary verbs, interrogatives, cardinal and ordinal numbers—words in universal use that furnish no evidence whatsoever for literary dependence. In addition, one finds the distinctive vocabulary of the New Testament in general. Such words as *Christ, Son of God, resurrection,* and *faith* must be excluded if our goal is to identify significant similarities in the vocabulary of the Synoptics that may show literary dependence.

To set this general New Testament vocabulary to the side and ensure that we arrive at defensible results, of the 830 words common to the Synoptics we leave out of consideration words that occur twenty times or more in the New Testament. This is a pragmatic decision; of course there may be cases in which a word occurs twenty times or more, but does so only in the Synoptics. Every reader is free to investigate whether this is the case by doing the detailed work that I choose not to undertake at this point. I strongly suspect, however, that closer scrutiny will alter my results very little.

Of the 830 words found in Matthew, Mark, and Luke, 494 words are found twenty times or more and should be counted as general New Testament vocabulary. That leaves 336 words common to the Synoptic Gospels that occur fewer than twenty times in the New Testament, 24.9 percent of Mark's vocabulary.

Closer investigation discloses that, of these 336 words, 105 occur in at least three other writings or groups of writings that make up the New Testament.[2] So, although the 105 words occur fewer than twenty times each, they are still part of the general vocabulary of the New Testament in terms of the range of documents in which they appear. Matthew and Luke would not have had to be dependent on Mark to use such words, and agreement in their use therefore furnishes no proof of a literary dependence.

Even usage

More important than how many of the 336 words belong to the general New Testament vocabulary because of their broad use outside the Synoptics is whether a word occurs among the Synoptics in an unbalanced or uneven fashion. This is frequently the case.

For example, imagine that Mark has a word eight times, Matthew once, and Luke five times. Imagine that Mark uses another word six times, Matthew twice, and Luke once. Or imagine again that Mark uses a word five times and Matthew and Luke just once or twice each. Such ratios better fit a theory of literary independence than one of dependence. Unless one unjustifiably assumes at the outset that Matthew and Luke were completely arbitrary, such cases require a sound explanation as to why Matthew and Luke—independent of each other—took so much offense at the Marcan word that they repeatedly replaced it in some cases, yet in other cases found it satisfactory enough to use. If nonparallelism occurs more often than parallelism, then it becomes most difficult to argue plausibly for literary dependence.

Yet each time Mark uses a word when Matthew and Luke do not, the nonparallelism in contrasting frequency offsets the par-

2. Following Morgenthaler, I group the Pauline, Petrine, and Johannine corpora as one group of writings each.

allelism in common usage. Such nonparallel use furnishes no additional evidence for literary dependence. If Matthew uses a word thirteen, nine, eight, seven, six, five, four, or three times, and Mark uses it only once, then no support is provided for literary dependence. Of course, one must reckon with the possibility that the greater frequency in Matthew is due to additional material in Matthew lacking in Mark. But if Matthew uses a word from two to twelve times when Mark does not use it at all, the one time Matthew does use it in parallel with Mark does not guarantee dependence. In any case the nonparallelism needs to be explained if one wishes to argue for literary dependence, for it far exceeds the parallelism, given the limited common use. Even where a word occurs in Matthew just once more than in Mark, the parallelism and nonparallelism cancel each other out.

The same goes for the relation between Mark and Luke. If Luke uses a word ten, seven, six, five, four, or three times, and Mark uses it just once, then the common occurrence offers no evidence of literary dependence. For the nonparallelism is larger than the parallelism. If a word occurs in Luke five times but in Mark only three times, or in any similar ratio, the nonparallelism still remains greater, or at best equal to, parallelism. No evidence for literary dependence is provided. *The only words that can be considered as evidence for literary dependence are those that occur in balanced fashion, or evenly, regardless of whether they are found in the three evangelists once, twice, three times, or more often.*

We are not maintaining, of course, that uneven occurrence could not be explained on the basis of the two-source theory or some other theory of literary dependence; explanations always can be devised to defend a theory once it has been asserted. The human intellect can think consistently. Indeed, from a purely theoretical standpoint it is eminently imaginable that, for example, Matthew took up a certain Marcan word twice and replaced it with another twice. But we are not justified in viewing such a possibility as established fact as long as we have not previously proven from better evidence that literary dependence exists. Otherwise we are engaged in constructing fantasy rather than in observing data. We deal here with the question of whether evidence justifies us to see a literary dependence at work. Only occurrences spread evenly through the three Synoptics furnish sound evidence.

The number of words that occur through the three Synoptics evenly, not counting general New Testament vocabulary, comes to seventy-two. Nine of these words name persons or places, knowledge of which need not have been transmitted in a common source document. Twenty words occur outside of the three Synoptics in two or three more writings or groups of writings. Thus they, too, must be counted as general New Testament vocabulary. Accordingly, forty-three words are left to investigate individually to determine whether they furnish a starting point for accepting a literary dependence among the three evangelists. Of these words, two occur four times, two occur three times, and three occur twice, so that in all there are fifty-six occurrences to consider.

The results of investigation are as follows:

1. Nineteen occurrences involve words of Jesus.
2. One is within a quotation from the Old Testament.
3. Nineteen are not parallel; that is, the occurrence is not in a parallel passage at all, or it is parallel in only two Gospels.
4. In fourteen occurrences the word is urged by the content of the pericope and could, therefore, have easily been used by all three authors independently. Three of these fourteen cases refer back to sayings of Jesus where this word was used previously.
5. Three words, each occurring once (numbers 10 [γαλήνη], 18 [καταγελᾶν], and 26 [ὁρμᾶν] in Fig. 7.2), permit consideration of literary dependence. *Based on the 1345 words of the Marcan vocabulary, that comes to 0.22 percent.* Nevertheless, we must first study each of these three words individually to test whether linguistic alternatives exist and whether the alternatives possess the same usability, given the linguistic and sociocultural context.

Of course anyone is at liberty to investigate the fourteen words that I take to be constituent components in the content of the pericope (point 4 above) in the same manner. Yet even if one wishes to advance the view that these fourteen permit an inference of literary dependence, there still would be quite small justification for inferring literary dependence among the three Synoptics. For these fourteen taken together comprise only 1.04 percent of Mark's vocabulary, and their seventeen occurrences amount to only 0.15 percent of the entire volume of Mark's Gospel.

Figure 7.2. Words Occurring Evenly in Matthew, Mark, and Luke, but Not Part of the General New Testament Vocabulary

Word	Number of Occurrences (Matt./Mark/Luke)	Parallel?	Types of occurrence
1. ἀγορά	3/3/3	1 ‖	J
2. ἄκρον		∦	
3. ἀλέκτωρ	3/3/3	1 ‖	1J/2RJ
4. ἀπαίρεσθαι			J
5. ἀποκυλίειν			S
6. ἄσβεστος			J
7. ἀσκός	4/4/4		J
8. βάθος		∦	
9. βδέλυγμα			J
10. γαλήνη			
11. γένημα			J
12. διαβλέπειν		∦	
13. δυσκόλως			J
14. εἰώθειν		∦	
15. ἐρήμωσις		∦	
16. ζημιοῦσθαι			J
17. θέρος			J
18. καταγελᾶν			
19. καταπέτασμα			S
20. καταρᾶσθαι		∦	
21. κατασκηνοῦν			J
22. κρανίον			P
23. κρημνός			S
24. μόδιος			J
25. ὄξος			S
26. ὁρμᾶν			
27. παίειν		∦	
28. παρασκευή		∦	
29. πατρίς	2/2/2	1 ‖	J
30. περίσσευμα		∦	

31. πονηρία		⊬	
32. πρίν	2/2/2		1J/2RJ
33. ῥήσσειν	2/2/2	1 ‖	J
34. σπόριμος			S
35. στέγη		⊬	
36. σῦκον		⊬	
37. συντηρεῖν		⊬	
38. τελώνιον			S
39. τίλλειν			S
40. τρίβος			OT
41. ὑπόκρισις		⊬	
42. φέγγος		⊬	
43. φραγμός		⊬	
44. χοῖρος	4/4/4		S

    J A word of Jesus
   RJ Referring to a word of Jesus
    P A place name
    S A word conditioned by the subject being treated
   OT Old Testament citation

    ‖ parallel
    ⊬ not parallel

Although not obligated to do so, we wish also to include words that are common between Mark and either Matthew or Luke.

Words Common to Matthew and Mark

Matthew, apart from Luke, has 189 words in common with Mark. The similarity in vocabulary between Matthew and Mark, accordingly, comes to 1019 words or 75.76 percent of the vocabulary of Mark's Gospel. That seems enormous at first glance, but of the 830 words shared by all three Synoptics it should be remembered that only three might be taken to support literary dependence. Likewise, one cannot go far in supporting current theories of literary dependence based on the agreement between Matthew and Mark alone.

Of the 189 words:

1. A total of 117 occur in an even fashion. Ten of the 117 occur twice, two occur three times, and two occur five times

each, so that the entire number of occurrences adds up to 139.

2. Sixty-five of these 139 occurrences involve Jesus' words and/or citations of the Old Testament; here, as already argued, the agreement is not necessarily conditioned by literary dependence.
3. Sixteen words occur in sentences that are not in parallel sentences but rather have different contents.
4. Five occurrences are names, which were not necessarily transmitted by written document.
5. Ten occurrences are words found outside of Matthew and Mark in three other writings or groups of writings; they should accordingly be seen as common New Testament vocabulary.
6. Twelve occurrences are conditioned by the content being presented.

That leaves thirty-one relevant occurrences, which consist of twenty-eight different words (Fig. 7.3). These words must, of course, be individually examined to determine whether there are linguistic alternatives and, if so, whether they possess the same usefulness as explanatory theories in terms of the linguistic and social context. If the verdict of such examination is positive, 2.08 percent of the vocabulary of Mark is eligible for explanation by literary dependence with Matthew. If one adds in the three relevant words shared by Matthew, Mark, and Luke, the percentage rises to 2.3 percent. That is not high for a hypothesis used as the foundation for one-third to one-half of New Testament theology!

Words Common to Mark and Luke

Luke by itself shares 106 more words in common with Mark, or a total of 109. Of these:

1. Sixty instances involving fifty-two words can be called usage in balanced fashion. Five of these words occur twice each; one word occurs four different times.
2. Two words with a total of three occurrences are found in three other writings or groups of writings.
3. Thirty-one occurrences are not parallel.

Figure 7.3.   Relevant Parallel Occurrences of Agreement Between Matthew and Mark

Word	Number of Occurrences (Matt./Mark)	Number of Relevant Parallels
1. ἀδημονεύειν	1/1	1
2. ἀρέσκειν	1/1	1
3. ἐνεργεῖν	1/1	1
4. θόρυβος	2/2	1
5. ἰχθύδιον	1/1	1
6. καταστρέφειν	1/1	1
7. καταχεῖν	1/1	1
8. κολαφίζειν	1/1	1
9. κτῆμα	1/1	1
10. λατομεῖν	1/1	1
11. μεταμορφοῦσθαι	1/1	1
12. παραλυτικός	5/5	3
13. πεζῇ	1/1	1
14. περιτιθέναι	3/3	2
15. πλέκειν	1/1	1
16. προσκυλίειν	1/1	1
17. προσλαμβάνεσθαι	1/1	1
18. πτῶμα	2/2	1
19. πυρέσσειν	1/1	1
20. σκεῖρα	1/1	1
21. σπυρίς	2/2	1
22. συσταυροῦν	1/1	1
23. τέκτων	1/1	1
24. ὑμνεῖν	1/1	1
25. φάντασμα	1/1	1
26. φραγελλοῦν	1/1	1
27. χωρίον	1/1	1
28. ψιχίον	1/1	1

Total, relevant parallel occurrences of agreement: 31

Among Matthew, Mark, and Luke

Word	Number of Occurrences (Matt./Mark/Luke)	Number of Relevant Parallels
1. γαλήνη	1/1/1	1
2. καταγελᾶν	1/1/1	1
3. ὁρμᾶν	1/1/1	1

Total, relevant occurrences of agreement: 3

Between Mark and Luke

Word	Number of Occurrences (Mark/Luke)	Number of Relevant Parallels
1. δύνειν	1/1	1
2. ἐπιτάσσειν	4/4	1
3. ἱματίζειν	1/1	1
4. κατακλᾶν	1/1	1
5. λαῖλαψ	1/1	1
6. νεότης	1/1	1
7. περικαλύπτειν	1/1	1
8. περικεῖσθαι	1/1	1
9. συσπαράπτειν	1/1	1
10. σωφρονεῖν	1/1	1
11. τρέμειν	1/1	1

Total, relevant parallel occurrences of agreement: 11

4. One occurrence involves a name, one quotes a saying of John the Baptist, and twelve cite words of Jesus or the Old Testament.
5. One occurrence is conditioned by the content that is being presented.

That leaves eleven relevant parallel occurrences. One of these, however (ἐπιτάσσειν in Fig. 7.3, "Between Mark and Luke"),

Figure 7.4.   A Summary of the 1345 Words that Make Up Mark's Vocabulary

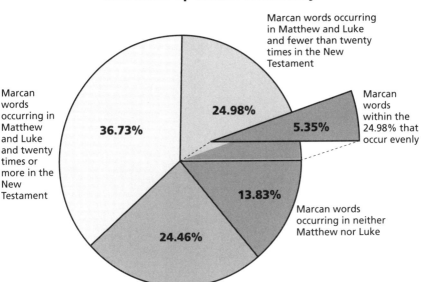

Marcan words occurring in Matthew and Luke and fewer than twenty times in the New Testament

Marcan words within the 24.98% that occur evenly

Marcan words occurring in Matthew and Luke and twenty times or more in the New Testament

Marcan words occurring in neither Matthew nor Luke

Marcan words occurring only in Matthew or Luke

24.98%

5.35%

36.73%

13.83%

24.46%

should be excluded, because its nonparallelism is far greater than its parallelism inasmuch as only one of its four occurrences is parallel. Accordingly, ten relevant words remain which Luke and Mark have in common; together with the three relevant words shared by Matthew, Mark, and Luke that makes 13, or 0.97 percent of the vocabulary of Mark that can be taken to affirm literary dependence between the Gospels of Luke and Mark (see Fig. 7.4). Who would be so bold as to base a hypothesis of literary dependence on this?

One can very well say that investigation of the extent of similarities in vocabulary among the three Synoptics turns up no significant agreement that could be viewed as evidence for literary dependence among them.

8

The Probability of Literary Dependence

Given the data collected in chapters 3 through 7, is literary dependence among the Synoptic Gospels probable? Before giving a final answer to that question, I would like to add one consideration to the development of our subject that has not been taken into account: What form could literary dependence take?

The scholars who assume literary dependence among the Synoptics have failed to describe what they mean when they speak of "dependence" and its implications. That lack of definition makes it possible to lump together numerous random and incompatible entities. But certain conditions and presuppositions are necessary for every form of literary dependence to occur. Dependence is conditioned by a specific mentality and gives rise to specific results. As a stimulus to thought along these lines Figure 8.1 and this chapter discuss seven forms of literary dependence. There may possibly be others; these are the ones I am aware of.

The Seven Forms of Dependence

The list in Figure 8.1 needs to be brought into dialogue with the results of chapters 3 through 7 in order to question whether those results support the presence of one of these forms of liter-

Figure 8.1. The Seven Forms of Dependence

	Copy	Précis	Quotation	Redactional reworking	Tendentious ideological/theological reworking	Plagiarism	Free reworking, creative rewriting
Precondition	Written exemplar is present.	Written exemplar is available only for a time.	Written exemplar is present, directly or remembered.	Written exemplar is present.	Written exemplar is present.	Written exemplar is present.	Exemplar may be an idea, common knowledge, literary.
Mentality	Literal copying intended.	Intention to record the essential content literally but in brief.	Intention to quote a short segment from another author.	Author views exemplar as correct (although allowing improvement)—otherwise the author would not bother with redaction.	Exemplar reproduced but pressed into the service of the redactor's own intention.	Theft of ideas; an author attempts to capitalize illicitly on the work of another.	Exemplar is used as starting point for free creation.
Probable outcome	Literal reproduction; copying mistakes possible; individual words may occasionally and instinctively be replaced with more familiar ones; extensive exact conformity to the exemplar.	Literal reproduction, shortening, at some points greater concision; never expansion; no stylistic improvement; no replacement of less desirable by more desirable words.	Exact conformity; only when citation is from memory are slight divergencies imaginable.	Linguistic and stylistic improvements, explanatory remarks on matters unknown to reader. Not expected: expansion or exchange of content or exchange of words, and rearrangement of sentences without improving them.	Exemplar altered, marked by a bias that can be sensed throughout. All incursions into original text are determined by this bias. Not expected: stylistic and linguistic alterations, polishing, exchanging words or additions having nothing to do with the bias.	Use of exemplar concealed as expeditiously as possible, so as to give the impression that no exemplar was used. Chapters rearranged; in sentences words are exchanged or the sentence construction itself is altered.	No exact conformity, literal reproduction, or identical content.

ary dependence. In this way the assessment of our results can be more objective. We now take up this task.

Copy

If a source is used, not only as a reference for dates or facts, but also so that its entire content is adopted, then one surely is dealing with literal reproduction or a copy. In the case of the Synoptic Gospels, however, the data clearly indicate that we are not dealing with copies: Apart from the words of Jesus, the literal agreement is far too small, as both our quantitative Synoptic comparison and our vocabulary investigation have shown. The lack of conformity in narrative order also goes against what one would expect in a copy.

Précis

According to the Griesbach hypothesis, Mark is a shortened summary of Matthew and Luke. Against this—in addition to the evident lack of literal agreement—is the considerable mass of minor details Mark adds: 2915 words (25.96 percent) of the Gospel in comparison to Matthew; 3343 words (29.77 percent) of the Gospel in comparison to Luke. Is it credible to posit that someone who wished to abridge his sources added more to his work than he extracted from them? In addition, in a précis one would not expect to find unique material.

Quotation

Citation as a form of literary dependence was included for the sake of completeness; but it fails to explain the Synoptic data and is accordingly not a major factor for purposes of this study.

Redactional Reworking

Editorial reworking would account for the linguistic differences insofar as they are linguistic improvements. Only a few of the linguistic differences between Matthew and Luke when compared to Mark, however, could be considered linguistic improvements. Mere assertions to the contrary, such as saying, "The differences are—*in Luke's eyes*—improvements." do not suffice. Redactional reworking does not explain all the data.

In general the great differences in word choice and the lack of additional minor details in Mark, as well as in Matthew and Luke, cannot be generally understood as redactional shortening

(*Kürzung*). This is particularly so when the minor additional details in Matthew and Luke, compared with Mark, remain unexplained. It makes no sense that redactors, who are supposed to have constantly restated what they found in their source in a more concise way, should have enlarged it throughout. Conversely, it seems unfounded to insist that a writer is dependent on a source when he demonstrates the capacity to add substantive information.

Tendentious Ideological/Theological Reworking

The data cannot be harmonized with theories that the author reworked an exemplar for theological reasons. Against such a theory is the connection of a source (for example, Mark in the two-source theory) with material of some other origin (for example, the non-Marcan material present in Matthew) once we move beyond isolated individual passages. Every enlargement would have to be attributable to the theological bias; the same goes for every difference from the exemplar except for unconscious alterations or possibly clear examples of linguistic improvement. But theories of redactional reworking cannot achieve this. Another stumbling stone here are the additional minor details of Mark compared to Matthew and Luke, as well as the additional minor details of Matthew or Luke compared to Mark. A final impediment are the great differences in wording and vocabulary (see chaps. 6 and 7).

Plagiarism

Justifiably, no one assumes the Gospels to be examples of plagiarism. The necessary conditions are absent: First, a plagiarized Gospel would have brought gain to no one. Second, the scope of each Gospel's coverage is too different; the plagiarist seeks fruit without labor, but enlarging and reducing the breadth of coverage would have required considerable effort. The additional minor details of the Gospels also defy what one would expect in the case of plagiarism.

Free Reworking, Creative Rewriting

The differences are great enough to make the thought of a new creative presentation plausible, but the data do not support such a theory. Against the idea of a rewrite is the agreement in content, which although not total is nevertheless substantial. Also against it is the uniform inclusion of additional material, for example the material common to Matthew and to Luke, which amounts to still more agreement in content. Also against it is the solid agreement within individual pericopes, despite their linguistic differences. Finally, by no means could such a theory explain the nearly 80 percent agreement in the words of Jesus.

Summary of Part 2

In view of the data in part 2, it is incumbent on anyone wishing to assert the literary dependence of the three Synoptics to demonstrate credibly a form of literary dependence consistent with these data. May no one think ill of me for harboring doubt that such a demonstration is possible.

In chapter 3 we learned that the material shared by Matthew and Mark comprises 55.46 percent of Matthew; material shared by Luke and Mark comprises 42.91 percent of Luke. Similarity in content is, however, no proof of literary dependence, for it could just as easily be due to historical rather than literary factors.

Chapter 4 showed that 50.43 percent of the three Synoptic Gospels follow a similar narrative sequence, 75.65 percent of the sequence in Matthew and Mark is similar, and 70.43 percent of the sequence in Mark and Luke is similar. This cannot, however, facilely be chalked up to literary dependence. The same results could as well be due to the actual sequence of the events reported. In favor of this is the almost seamless similarity in the passion and resurrection accounts, where the order of events is substantially conclusive.

Chapter 5 identified the extent of parallelism between Matthew and Mark at 46.5 percent, and between Mark and Luke at 36.17 percent, based on the entire Gospel of Mark.

Chapter 6's quantitative cross-sectional Synoptic investigation showed that only 22.17 percent of the words examined that are parallel in all three Synoptics are totally identical. In Matthew and Mark the amount is 40.99 percent; in Luke and Mark it is 34.29 percent. The differences in wording of parallel verses come to 95.68 percent in Matthew and Mark and 100.43 percent in Mark and Luke. Such data do not favor literary dependence among the three Synoptics.

Of course, it is possible here and there to point to half and occasionally entire sentences containing literal agreement in at least two of the three Synoptics. This is possible even outside the words of Jesus, which occupy a special position. But such agreement is rare. Only exceptionally does it cover an entire verse, and it never goes so far as to cover an entire pericope.

Chapter 7 made clear that no literary dependence can be based on significant similarities in vocabulary, which come to 0.22 percent of Mark compared to the other two, to 2.3 percent for Mark and Matthew, and to 0.97 percent for Mark and Luke.

In view of these data, I would like to ask whether the reader is willing to continue to hold to the assumption of literary dependence among the three Synoptic Gospels. *If there is no proof for literary dependence then it makes no sense to offer theories to tell who was dependent on whom.* It is true that the two-source theory has become a habit of thought, but those stalwarts who refuse to be dissuaded from clinging to the two-source theory should consider the data which speak against their assumption:

The advocate of the two-source theory regards literal agreement among the three Gospels as evidence for literary dependence, so the minor agreements between Matthew and Luke against Mark are a considerable problem. I have counted 258 such minor agreements myself, and I doubt that I have found them all.[1]

Similarly, the additional minor details present a problem for the two-source advocate in both directions. One must, for example, explain why Matthew shortened the pericopes he took from Mark by 2915 words or 28.01 percent of their total, yet at the same time added 2270 words, or 21.82 percent to them (see p. 104). One blanket explanation might account for either situation alone, but hardly for both together. The advocate would also be responsible for explaining why Matthew failed to include thirteen Marcan pericopes.

With respect to Luke, one must account for the omission of no fewer than twenty-four pericopes and at the same time explain

1. See the list in Hans-Herbert Stoldt, *History and Criticism of the Marcan Hypothesis* (Macon, Ga.: Mercer University Press, 1980), 18–21. I will not produce my own list here but refer rather to the last section of Fig. 6.6 (p. 119–27), which allows a projection. In reexamining the evidence I have already discovered still more literal agreement between Matthew and Luke.

why Luke shortened the pericopes he relied on by 3343 words, or 38.19 percent of their length. Yet at the same time the writer expanded them by 1330 words or 15.19 percent of their original extent (see pp. 103–5).

Also in need of explanation are the marked differences among the Synoptics in how they formulate their common material. These differences run to something like 100 percent, while similarities in the wording of the common material are, at most, 40 percent when comparing two Gospels (see pp. 128–29).

Sworn advocates of the Griesbach hypothesis are in no better position than classic two-source proponents, however, in view of the results of our investigation. If they give up Griesbach's corollary, the dependence of Luke on Matthew,[2] then they can make no claim to have solved the Synoptic problem as it has been understood and presented around the world. If they feel they must argue for literary dependence to account for the relationship of Mark to Matthew and Luke due to the similarities, how can they manage to account for the similarities between Luke and Matthew without Griesbach's corollary?

The agreement between these two Gospels is, however, much greater than their respective agreements with Mark, since they share not only the material common to all three Synoptics but also the material common only to Matthew and Luke. Then one must factor in the additional minor details lacking in Mark but present in Matthew and Luke (see p. 108). In view of this, if one accounts for Luke's Gospel without accepting literary dependence (that is, gives up Griesbach's corollary), what justification does one have for asserting literary dependence for Mark's Gospel?

The problem of the additional minor details presents the Griesbach hypothesis with even greater problems than it presents the two-source theory: By Griesbach reckoning, Mark must have added to his sources both the 258 additional minor details, containing 2013 words that his sources lacked, as well as the 902 additional words lacking in Matthew and the 1330 additional words lacking in Luke. That makes 4245 words, or 37.80 percent of Mark's Gospel (see pp. 27, 28, 102). At the same time, in the wording of the pericopes he adopted he must have obliterated the 2270 words of Matthew's additional minor details as well as

2. Cf. Stoldt, *History and Criticism*,. 239–64.

the 1324 words of Luke's. That is a total of 3594 words, or an amount equal to 32.01 percent of Mark's Gospel. Mark must also have rearranged the 7839 words (69.81 percent of his Gospel) that he took from his sources (see p. 107). That doesn't even count different word choice and verbal form nor different sentence construction he must have employed. In addition, by his selection of pericopes he must have reduced his two sources by about one-half; none of the important pericopes that make up the unique material in Matthew and Luke found grace in Mark's sight (see pp. 98, 107). He must have used the pericopes that he did take over from his two sources in such an absurd fashion that he—to the extent that he could not fall back on formulations that his sources had in common—picked up alternately one, two, or three words from Matthew and from Luke, and then inserted a few words of his own.

Only someone who is keen to put up with such absurdities can continue to hold to the Griesbach hypothesis rather than opting for the alternative—bidding farewell, finally, to the unproved and unprovable claim of literary dependence among the three Synoptic Gospels.

One does not get around the problem by regarding Mark "as a novel representation of Matthew and Luke in narrative form."[3] That is an empty assertion, not falsifiable and therefore also not verifiable (see p. 27). It contradicts ancient church claims to the contrary and replaces reliable testimony with poetic license. That is too high a price to pay for the privilege of calling the more comprehensive Matthew original instead of the shorter Mark.

In conclusion we need only state that, not only the two-source theory but also the Griesbach hypothesis, with their underlying assertion of literary dependence among the three Synoptic Gospels, are both finished when the Synoptic data has been sifted. No room remains for free-floating hypotheses.

---

3. Ibid, p. 259. Stoldt characterizes Griesbach's view this way.

Part 3

Could the Synoptic Gospels Have Arisen Independently?

9

The Possibility
of Understanding
the Synoptic Gospels
Without Literary Dependence

Building on what we have learned about the Synoptic Gospels, we now take up two pressing questions that our findings require us to discuss: First, is it possible to understand all the data of the Synoptics without accepting literary dependence among them? That will be the focus of chapter 9. Second, if there was no literary dependence then how did the Synoptic Gospels arise? This question will be discussed in chapter 10.[1]

The Challenge to Investigate

The lack of evidence for literary dependence among the three Synoptic Gospels is overwhelming and speaks for itself. Anyone who remains unconvinced may nevertheless undertake to negate the results at which we arrived. This could be done in various ways.

1. See in relation to this whole chapter Franz Stuhlhofer, *Jesus und seine Schüler. Wie zuverlässig wurden Jesu Worte überliefert?* (Gießen/Basel: Brunnen, 1991); David C. C. Watson, *Fact or Fantasy? The Authenticity of the Gospels* (Worthing, England: J. E. Walter, 1980). These works were not accessible to me until after the present book was complete; since then I have noted numerous commonalities.

An investigation could determine the number of instances of stereotypical figures of speech in everyday language used to pass on the same content within the same socio-cultural context. We will explain more about these speech patterns later in this chapter. The number of stereotypes in analogous writings could be quantified and calculations made regarding the established transitional usage[2] of individual words, whose occurrence is conditioned by the content,[3] forming part of the linguistic pattern that occurs. The findings could be compared with the Synoptics.

Besides this linguistic approach comparable material could be investigated. True, the Gospels are singular; no other writings grow from a relationship totally analogous to the relationships these writers enjoyed with the one whose words, deeds, and suffering they report. Still, material does exist, or could be generated, for formal comparison.

One could, for example, compare the Synoptics in content and vocabulary with examples of retold stories. I have in mind here a class assignment involving a statistically significant number of students who retell given stories to one another. The predictable result would be both similarities and differences in for-

2. ["Established transitional usage" translates Linnemann's word *Übergangswahrscheinlichkeit*. She explains that this is "a technical expression used in the case of words that combine with certain other words to form set formulations. It plays a role in cognitive psychology. Some examples: In German we have the term *Untersuchung* (*investigation*). In theory this term could be used with various verbs, but in practice it is common to say: 'to conduct an investigation' (*eine Untersuchung anstellen*). We say, then, that there is a high degree of established transitional usage between *investigation* and *conduct*. Further, one could in theory link *investigation* with adjectives such as *accurate*, *precise*, or *exact*. But in practice one normally speaks only of an *accurate* investigation (*eine genaue Untersuchung*). The established transitional usage (*Übergangswahrscheinlichkeit*) of *investigation* in connection with *accurate* is greater than with *precise* or other words. Another example: *lepers* are regarded as *unclean*. We can therefore figure on a high degree of established transitional usage between the word *leprosy* (*Aussatz*) and *unclean* (*unrein*) or *purify* (*reinigen*), while the established transitional usage between *leprosy* and *cure* (*heilen*) is extremely slight. The point to be made with respect to synoptic usage is this: when a pair of words occurs in the New Testament that have a high degree of established transitional usage (like *leprosy* and *purify*), that is not a two-fold proof of literary dependence. For the conjunction of those two words is rather a matter of established transitional usage (*Übergangswahrscheinlichkeit*)."]

3. A word that is conditioned by, or closely connected with, certain content may most usually appear with certain other words to form a set formulation, a stereotypical usage. Such a formulation is also no proof of literary dependence, for it owes its existence rather to a linguistic stereotype.

mulations in the resulting versions of these stories. One could quantify the similarities and differences for each individual assignment and then calculate in cross-section an average for all of them. Assuming that the percentages of similarities turned out to be markedly lower than the percentages arrived at for the Gospels, one could regard this as proof of literary dependence among the Gospels.

In other words, in view of the results of my work, it is quite risky to continue to assert literary dependence among the Gospels. If one insists on doing so, one ought to move beyond mere assertions and attempt to furnish proof using comparable material. What I am interested in here, then, are possible ways to falsify my investigation. Only that which can be falsified may be regarded, at least in principle, as also being verifiable.[4]

One could investigate eyewitness statements about traffic accidents, in which a statistically relevant number of cases would be required to form a reliable data basis. One could also examine differences in medical reports describing the same malady. A medical report is compiled for every patient receiving care in a hospital. Over the years thousands of reports gather, and filing systems make it possible, without too much difficulty, to sort out all reports of a certain illness. Since in a hospital several doctors are active at the same time on rotation, so independent reports of the same illness as described by different doctors are available. Since every illness and its treatment involves the use of a specific technical vocabulary, one can count on literal agreement in the reports, as well as differences.[5]

4. I refer here to a principle of positivistic philosophy, which holds that assertions are irrelevant if they cannot be falsified. What cannot be falsified can also not be verified and therefore cannot be regarded as verified. Only assertions, or research results in the form of assertions, that are in principle fundamentally falsifiable (which does not mean that they must turn out to be false in fact!) are relevant. Therefore I consider it important that ways be shown of possible falsification of my results.

5. The analogies of medical reports and retold stories comprise formal parallels. They call attention to the fact that literal agreement in comparable material is by no means extraordinary but an entirely normal phenomenon that we encounter daily. If one wishes to use literal agreement as a sign of literary dependence, then one must first clarify the extent to which such literal agreement exceeds that which one can expect when no literary dependence is involved. Literal agreement does not justify a priori assertion of literary dependence; one must first ask: is the extent of literal agreement so great as to necessitate literary dependence to explain it?

Presumably there are numerous other possibilities. The point would be to determine whether the percentage of similarities in word order and vocabulary in material arising from the same content and comparable context is significantly lower than we have established for the Synoptic Gospels. There is, however, an extra consideration that must be factored in, due to the generally high degree of precision with which Jesus' words have been passed on: only pericopes that do not quote Jesus' words would actually be comparable.

Anyone who does not trust the results of my investigation thus far—that there is no proof for literary dependence among the Synoptics—should not simply express an opinion to the contrary. That person should rather get to work and investigate comparable material so that evidence accessible to the unbiased observer (besides Synoptic material, which is the evidence in question) can be shown to support proposed explanations of Synoptic dependence. Unfortunately, however, I suspect that there will be a strong tendency to continue to hold to the theory of literary dependence among the Gospels without even an attempt at the falsification of these findings. The reason is not that the results are unconvincing, but rather that they do not fit in with established views [They fall outside the edifice of conceptions depicted in Fig. 1.2 (see p. 24) and so may be safely ignored.].

Literary Dependence and Worldview

If one insists that Jesus said or did few of the things reported of him in the Gospels, then some kind of theory of literary dependence is necessary. Under this presupposition, what the Gospels report about Jesus is nothing but literature—made-up words of Jesus and made-up stories about his actions. That the Gospel writers, independent of one another, made up the same stories and sayings two or even three times is quite improbable; no such phenomenon can be substantiated in the history of literature. So under this presupposition, literary dependence is indispensable, for it permits one to understand the second, third, or even fourth version of given material as dependent on one original document. This presupposition, though, is patently arbitrary. It is rooted neither in the Gospel data nor in the ancient historical testimony about the Gospels, but rather on a concept of history derived from a monistic worldview.

Accepting a monistic worldview as binding is a faith decision by which one, consciously or unconsciously, contradicts faith in God as the Creator and Ruler of history and in his redemptive work. This contradiction invariably results in the continual discovery of contradictions in the revealed Word of God—simply because one is standing in personal contradiction to him.

The monistic worldview presupposes that only one world— the visible world—exists. The concept of history based on this worldview defines a *historical* event as an event analogous with other normal, everyday events. It can be traced back to preceding events; it can be understood from its reciprocal relationship with contemporaneous factors. This kind of concept of history, which acknowledges truth only in that which can be established inductively, has no place for revelation; advocates of this concept of history interpret any testimony concerning the unseen world as a "tall tale."

The person ruled by such a concept of history is forced to do violence to the New Testament, and to the Old Testament as well. Scripture must not be allowed to say what it says. No one should be surprised that applications of "methods" based on this concept of history lead to absurdities.

The Event and the Record

The empirical data give persons who have no faith commitment to a monistic worldview no reason to accept literary dependence among the Synoptic Gospels.

Clearly the Gospels intend to report the words and deeds, as well as the suffering, of Jesus Christ, the Son of God. This is evident in every pericope; it is expressly stated in Luke 1:1–4. What historical-critical exegesis rejects as "historicizing"—taking what is reported in the Gospels as historical—is, therefore, a legitimate approach to the Gospels: *Behind what the Gospels report stand the words and deeds of Jesus.* That is the source of similarities in content and sequence of the pericopes. The Gospels all have the same foundation: What Jesus said, did, and suffered; that led inevitably to similarities in content.

But it also necessarily led to differences for this reason: *Every event is more comprehensive than attempts to embody it in words can convey.* Not only the deeds but also the suffering of Jesus, indeed even his words are, structurally, events. Every event has a complex structure, as depicted in Figure 9.1, step 1. It encompasses:

1. the course of the event—action, result, reaction;
2. the external framework—place and time, situation, accompanying circumstances, as well as the (various) participants, and
3. the inner connections:
   a. of the acting agent to the action, to the various participants, and to the entire framework of the action;
   b. of various other participants to the acting agent, to the actions, to other participants, to factors outside of the event.

No attempt to embody an event in words can grasp the fullness of these implications unless a whole book were devoted to one individual event; even then there is no guarantee that an event's comprehensive totality would be conveyed.

In considering a verbal record or deposit (for example, of an

Figure 9.1.   The Linguistic Fixing of the Gospels

Step 1: The Event Occurs and Is Remembered.

Event (Word, Deed, or Suffering)

1. *The course of the event*—action, result, reaction.
2. *The external framework*—place and time, situation, accompanying circumstances, participants.
3. *The inner connections of the acting agent* to the action, to various other participants, and to the framework of the action.
4. *The inner connections of various other participants* to the acting agent, to the actions, to one another, to factors outside of the event.

event), we must therefore distinguish between what is *direct* and what is *indirect* [communication]. Words [for example, Jesus' teachings] are fixed linguistic symbols; they can be transmitted *directly.* A deed, on the other hand, must be fixed [encoded into words] or recorded linguistically before it can be passed along. If there is no literary dependence, then any recording into linguistic form is *original. Variants* in the account of an event by various eyewitnesses are, therefore, normal. Complete agreement in formulation, in contrast, points to dependence, as every criminal investigator takes into account when questioning witnesses.

Yet there should be substantial agreement among witnesses. If the same event is reported, there *must* be agreement of some kind. Such agreement is, of course, considerably greater in the case of a direct linguistic record, since the linguistically fixed form does not first have to be found. Similar agreement can, however, be readily recognized in the case of an indirect linguistic record as it transmits the course, framework, and connections of an event.

All this holds true, obviously, with agreement in content; but even verbal agreement is by no means unusual. Although a language's vocabulary may run from fifty thousand to one hundred thousand words, people normally use only a fraction of that. The amount varies, often according to socio-economic class (A few years ago, if I remember correctly, a linguist determined that the average active vocabulary among the lower socio economic class was just 600 words.). The same words are generally used for varying objects or phenomena,[6] even though the language may have many other words that could serve as well. These words combine in stereotyped expressions.[7]

The linguistic fixing of an event (apart from direct communication) does not occur, as a rule, while the event takes place, but later, when it is remembered. The way it is transformed into language is determined:

6. [Linnemann explains with this example: a number of words can refer to a basic activity like walking (*gehen*)—to wander, to stride, to stroll, to propel oneself forward, etc. (*wandeln, schreiten, spazieren, sich fortbewegen*, etc.). But there is often just one particular word in common, regular use.]

7. As far as I can see, the phenomenon of linguistic stereotyping has still barely been researched, although if one is alert one encounters it constantly in everyday usage.

1. *through the medium of language.* Language is concrete in that every language has set characteristics in vocabulary, structure, general stereotypical usage, and basic patterns that reflect specific socio-cultural conditions.

2. *through the one who formulates the words.* Factors here include the communicator's personal characteristics, socio-cultural background, mastery of the language, choice about what level of language is used, fluency, relation to the event and to active participants in the event, and the perspective of the eyewitnesses.

Both sets of factors are at work in putting the memories into a linguistic record. In biblical pericopes we may not forget the most important factor of all—the Holy Spirit makes use of all the factors listed above (see Fig. 9.1, step 2).

The linguistic fixing of the words, deeds, and suffering of Jesus occurred primarily in the same language, colloquial Aramaic, that Jesus himself used. That applies not only for the original version of Matthew's Gospel, which was written in Aramaic,[8] but also for the content of Mark's Gospel, which was originally fixed orally in Peter's native Aramaic tongue.[9] Since Luke procured his information from eyewitnesses (Luke 1:2), the original linguistic fixing of the content of his Gospel also took place in Aramaic. The memories of Jesus' words, deeds, and suffering were linguistically fixed, therefore, in the same medium and concrete language and under the same conditions. The linguistic fixing also occurred among those who shared eyewitness status and a similar relation to Jesus as Messiah and Lord. All this necessarily resulted in similarities in the way these memories were formulated. In addition, we must assume there were modifications and assimilations as disciples shared and exchanged their common reminiscences after Jesus' ascension in Jerusalem.

The integrity of our knowledge of all this could appear shaky in view of the fact that the Gospels have been transmitted in

8. See pp. 187–89.
9. Cf. ibid. Of course this is not to argue that Peter was translated by Mark from Aramaic into Latin in Rome, although that is possible; it is merely to declare that Peter's reminiscences were linguistically fixed in his mother tongue, although he also had facility in Koine Greek.

Figure 9.1   The Linguistic Fixing of the Gospels

Step 2: Direct and Indirect Material from the Event Contributes to a Linguistic Deposit.

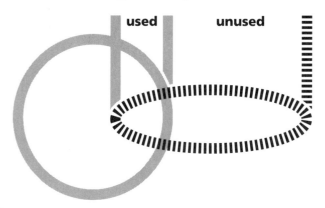

used   unused

Direct: Transmission of words.

Indirect: Transmission of the course of events, external framework, and inner connections.

The linguistic conception of the memory of an event is determined:

1. *Through the medium of language.* Language is concrete. Each language has its own set characteristics in vocabulary and structure, in general stereotypical usage, and in basic patterns.
2. *Through the one who formulates the words.* Operative factors here include personal characteristics, socio-cultural background, mastery of language, level of language used, fluency, relation to the event and to the active agent in the event, and the perspective of the eyewitnesses.
3. *Through the Holy Spirit,* who uses 1 and 2.

Greek, not Aramaic. But this does not matter as much as one might assume at first view:

1. In no small measure the language into which a book is translated is nevertheless dominated by the original language—often to its detriment. This is observable in books translated from other languages (such as the English edition of the book you are now reading). At least in part, the linguistic structures of the Aramaic original might be pre-

Figure 9.1.   The Linguistic Fixing of the Gospels

Step 3: Variants in the Linguistic Deposit Appear As Others Develop Their Own Linguistic Conceptions.

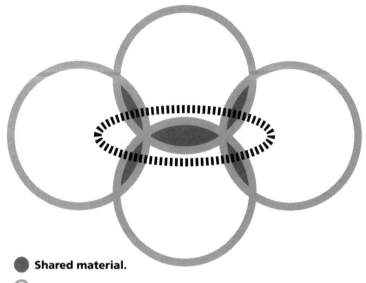

● **Shared material.**

○ **Unique material.**

1. Every event is more comprehensive than any possible linguistic deposit describing or referring to it.
2. Variants in the linguistic deposit are normal.
3. Agreement among the variants is normal.

served in translation, creating a number of coincidental agreements.[10]

2. Mark's Gospel was not written by someone whose mother tongue was *koine* Greek, but rather by someone who was at home in Aramaic. The Aramaic version of Matthew probably also was translated into Greek from the mother tongue, since it is highly improbable that someone who was comfortable in Greek, the language understood everywhere, would have taken the trouble to acquire such a powerful mastery of Aramaic. If both Gospels are written in translation Greek, similarities in formulation must be reckoned

10. Cf. the investigations of Adolf Schlatter on the language of the Gospels.

with. It is true that Aramaic was not Luke's native language, but one cannot rule out the possibility that the Aramaic formulations of the eyewitness reports he gathered come through in his Greek writings.

3. In Greek-speaking Christian circles the Septuagint was used. This must have led to assimilations in language.

4. Since Christian communities had various and diverse connections among one another, one must suppose that, in short order, a common Christian basic vocabulary emerged. In other words, the phraseology of faith, so to speak, of one group might be taken over quickly by another. This process is observable on the mission field today.

The similarities among the three Synoptic Gospels—which in any case are not overly great—are, therefore, thoroughly understandable without recourse to acceptance of literary dependence.

Other Issues

Are there not, however, still problems in the Synoptic Gospels, despite all I have said above, problems like 1) topical rather than historical arrangement,[11] 2) variants, 3) differences in sequence, 4) summaries that furnish sure proof of literary dependence, 5) striking verbal agreements, and most of all 6) the uniform basic construction of all three Gospels? Below we consider each of these five areas in turn.

11. [The German word is *Sachordnung*. Linnemann refers to the common view that the sequence of pericopes in the Gospels is not necessarily due to historical occurrence but rather to the topical or thematic interest of the writer or compiler. Like is combined with like: miracle story with miracle story, parable with parable, and so on. This means that there are, for example, topically arranged parables and miracle stories that violate the—ostensible—historical order as it actually took place. In historical–critical exegesis one says: "When several miracle stories follow each other, this does not mean that Jesus performed these miracles one after another, but that these pericopes are arranged topically rather than historically."] If pericopes of the same kind appear as a sequence, then historical critical theology alleges a topical arrangement. In such cases it is taken for granted that the sequence is not the result of following the course of events but is a literary arrangement. It is argued that Jesus could not be supposed to have for some time of his life only worked miracles and in other times done nothing but pass on parables. Therefore, topical arrangement is used as an argument that the Gospels are not biographies of Jesus.

Topical Arrangement

How are we to understand the phenomenon of topical rather than historical arrangement, if we assume that the Synoptic Gospels convey what Jesus said and did? Is the shared arrangement of material, for example parables and miracle accounts, understandable apart from literary dependence?

Parables

We cannot really speak of any thoroughgoing conformity in the ordering of parables in Mark, Matthew, or Luke. Mark relates two parables in chapter 2 and four in chapter 4; in one of these four an interpretation is added. There is one parable each in chapters 12 and 13, respectively. Only half of all Marcan parables are found, therefore, in chapter 4.

In Matthew we find two parables in chapter 5, one in chapter 7, and two in chapter 9. Seven parables appear in chapter 13, two in chapter 18, and one in chapter 20. In chapter 21 there are two, in chapters 22 and 24 one each, and in chapter 25 three. Less than one-third of the parables of Matthew appear in chapter 13, the parable chapter that is alleged to be arranged by *Sachordnung*, the gathering together of materials of the same kind. But there are fifteen other parables, more than twice as many as found in chapter 13, distributed through the rest of Matthew's Gospel.

Luke looks very much the same: Two parables stand in chapter 5, one each in chapter 6 and 7. Two additional parables are found in chapter 8, one in chapter 10, and two in chapter 11. In chapters 13, 14, and 15 we find three parables each, respectively; in chapter 16 there are two. In chapter 17 we read one, in 18 two, and in 19, 20, and 21 just one each.

Of Luke's twenty-nine parables, only two parallel Jesus' celebrated parable Sermon by the Sea (Mark 4). Of the seven parables parallel to Mark 4 in Matthew, Jesus spoke four of them to the multitude and three to the disciples. If one adds up the parables that, according to the three Gospels, were spoken to the multitude in the same sermon, the total is five, all of which are rooted in the same subject matter: sowing and harvest. Given the setting of a sermon that is realistic; there is no need to understand it as an order imposed on the material at some future time.

Miracle Accounts

When one scrutinizes the miracle accounts one discovers the same thing: There is little overall topical or thematic ordering as such to be found in the Synoptic Gospels.

Of the eighteen miracles that Mark reports (apart from summaries), three are in chapter 1; one each in chapters 2, 3 and 4; three in chapter 5, and one in chapter 6. Chapters 7 and 8 contain two each, while there is one each in chapters 9, 10, and 11.

Matthew's miracle accounts are distributed thus: five each in chapters 8 and 9, two each in chapters 12, 14, 15, and 17. Chapters 20 and 21 record one miracle account each.

Luke's twenty miracles appear over a span of twelve chapters: two in chapter 4, three in chapter 5, one in chapter 6, two in chapter 7, four in chapter 8, two in chapter 9, and then one each in chapters 11, 13, 14, 17, 18, and 22. Here also, therefore, there can be no talk of overwhelmingly similar topical ordering of material.

The distribution of the miracle accounts tends on the whole to cast doubt on, rather than to support, literary dependence. There is no unambiguous *Sachordnung* in the three Gospels whose existence could only be explained by literary dependence.

Variants

How are we to understand the phenomenon of variants? Although divergences in formulation and differences in individual statements can be explained by allowing for the various perspectives of eyewitnesses, there are still divergences to be accounted for in comparable pericopes for which the explanation of eyewitness perspective falls short. An example is the beatitudes in the Sermon on the Mount (Matt. 5:3–12), on the one hand, and in the Sermon on the Plain (Luke 6:20–26), on the other. Another example would be the parable of the royal wedding (Matt. 22:1–14), on the one hand, and the great banquet (Luke 14:15–24), on the other. Are we not forced in these instances to posit the reworking of a written exemplar or at least the reshaping of a tradition? Surely both elements in these so-called *doublets* are not somehow equally original, are they?

In order to answer this question correctly, one should not forget that someone who has a message to proclaim, and who proclaims it itinerantly in various places, will likely not proclaim it in just one form everywhere he speaks. He will rather vary the message in view of the specific situations of the various settings and persons he addresses. The itinerant nature of Jesus' speaking ministry should in itself prepare us to expect differing versions. Besides, there is no reason why he should not have performed the same kind of miracle more than once.

Variation in Sequence of Pericopes

How can we explain differences in sequence of pericopes that present the same incidents? Do such differences not amount to contradictions, invalidating the view that the same course of events forms the background for the Gospels?

In answering this question we should note that variations in sequence can have a number of causes. First, in Mark's case we must observe that his order does not intend to pass along the actual historical sequence in every case. Papias (writing ca. A.D. 98–117[12]) appears to have touched on this when he wrote:

> And the Presbyter used to say this, "Mark became Peter's interpreter and wrote accurately all that he remembered, not, indeed, in order, of the things said or done by the Lord. For he had not heard the Lord, nor had he followed him, but later on, as I said, followed Peter, who used to give teaching as necessity demanded but not making, as it were, an arrangement of the Lord's oracles . . ."[13]

Second, the Gospels claim to report only a portion of all that Jesus said and did. An inevitable result is that their reports will sometimes vary in sequence. Consider: The length of Jesus' public ministry is generally given as three years. If one compares the time span of his activity to the literary record of the Gospels the inescapable conclusion is that the Gospels preserve only a portion of Jesus' sayings and actions (Note here John 21:25.).

Three years—that is 1095 days. If one sets aside, say, 95 days to cover such times as the forty days in the wilderness, passion week, and the like, when Jesus was not active in proclaiming and

---

12. Papias' date is widely disputed and often placed near the middle of the second century. But an earlier date seems required by the full range of evidence: see Robert Yarbrough, "The Date of Papias: A Reassessment," in *Journal of the Evangelical Theological Society* 26.2 (1983): 181–91.

13. Eusebius *Ecclesiastical History* 3.39.15.

working miracles, that leaves 1000 days. Let us suppose that Jesus' average time of public proclamation was two hours daily (probably a low estimate). That makes 2000 hours. Jesus was with his disciples day and night; it is thus certainly not improbable that we should allow for another two hours of instruction for the disciples each day. If one were to type out the transcript of what someone says in two hours of discourse, one would end up with no less than fifteen single-spaced typewritten pages. So a conservative estimate of what Jesus said publicly might be the equivalent of 15,000 typed pages. He spoke another 15,000 pages to his closest followers. That makes 30,000 typed pages. Two hundred such pages is the length of a medium-sized book; that means Jesus spoke the equivalent of some 150 books. But these would contain just what he said. They would hold nothing by way of describing Jesus' miracles. Probably it would be far too low an estimate to suppose that for the 1000 days, Jesus was involved in such works for an average of one-half hour daily. That would give a total of 500 hours to relate, if one were writing all about Jesus' ministry.

Only thirty-five miracles are attested, however, one of these four times and ten of them three times. Seven miracles appear in two Gospels each, while seventeen of them occur in only one Gospel.[14]

In view of the wealth of possible material, and the fact that each Gospel is selective in what it relates, so that in many cases there are no parallels in other Gospels to what one Gospel re-

---

14. The feeding of the five thousand is attested four times. Attested three times (Matt.-Mark-Luke): the stilling of the storm, the healing of the leper, the Garasene demonic, blind Bartimaeus, the woman with a hemorrhage, the epileptic son, the lame man, Peter's mother-in-law, the man with a withered hand, Jairus' daughter. Attested two times: the feeding of the four thousand (Matthew–Mark), the cursing of the fig tree (Matthew–Mark), the daughter of the Syro-Phoenician woman (Matthew–Mark), the blind and dumb demonic (Matthew–Luke), the synagogue leader from Capernaum (Mark–Luke), walking on the water (Matthew–John), the demonic in the synagogue (Mark–Luke). Attested once in Matthew: coin in the fish's mouth, a dumb demonic, two blind men. Attested once in Mark: a blind man in Bethsaida, a deaf and dumb man. Attested once in Luke: Peter's catch, ten lepers, Malchus' ear, crippled woman, a man with dropsy, the widow of Nain's son. Attested once in John: wedding at Cana, catch of fish after the resurrection, man born blind, man paralyzed for 38 years, son of a royal official, Lazarus.

ports, differences in sequence are a necessary and unavoidable result.

Third, differences in sequence could always arise when the same thing is reported more than once and the reports of Jesus' words in parallel passages goes back to different renderings of what Jesus said on various occasions.

Summaries

How can we make sense of summaries of pericopes that are said to furnish proof for literary dependence? Passages often cited include Mark 1:14–15; 1:32–34; 3:7–12; 4:33–34, and 6:53–56 and their parallels. These are said not to be tradition but redaction—Matthew and Luke could only have derived their versions of these incidents from the source (i.e. Mark) they had before them.

Let us consider each of the above five Marcan passages in turn:

Mark 1:14–15

Matthew 4:12 and Luke 4:14a, which parallel Mark 1:14–15, agree with Mark 1:14a in only three words. Luke 4:14a does not even vaguely agree in content with its parallels; Luke 4:14b has no agreement at all. Matthew 4:13–16 is unique, as is Luke 4:15.

Only between Mark 1:14b–15 and Matthew 4:17 is there similarity in both form and content: five of twenty-three words are identical, or 21.74 percent of the words in Mark. Yet if the Marcan and Matthean pericopes are compared in their entirety, only eight words of the thirty-five in Mark are identical to the words found in Matthew. That is 22.86 percent verbal agreement—but dissimilarities come to ninety-three words, or 265.71 percent. This makes literary dependence improbable. No literary exemplar was required for Matthew (or Luke) to pass along the crucial message that Jesus proclaimed from village to village in Galilee.

Mark 1:32–34

Of forty-six words in Mark 1:32–34 only a single *and* (*kai*) is identical in Matthew-Mark-Luke. That is a verbal agreement of 2.17 percent. Matthew and Mark alone share nine more words in total agreement, as do Mark and Luke. That makes a total of ten, or 21.74 percent. Matthew has fifty-two differences (113.04 percent compared with Mark), Luke sixty-two (134.78 percent compared with Mark). The differences are even more numerous than usual. Such data render a literary dependence highly improbable.

Mark 3:7–12

Of 103 words in Mark 3:7–12, only one is identical in Matthew-Mark-Luke. That is just 0.97 percent. Matthew-Mark have eleven more words in common, or twelve in all, which makes 11.65 percent total agreement when compared with Mark. Mark-Luke have eight words in common, or nine in all, which makes 8.74 percent total agreement compared with Mark's 103 words. The differences between Mark and Matthew come to 136, or 132.04 percent of Mark, and between Mark and Luke 124, or 120.39 percent of Mark. These differences are, therefore, far above average. They do not speak in favor of literary dependence.

Mark 4:33–34

Regarding Mark 4:33–34: there is no parallel in Luke. Of the 25 words in Mark, five are matched by Matthew, but the differences number 45, or 180 percent—no proof of literary dependence.

Mark 6:53–56

A Lucan parallel to Mark 6:53–56 is utterly lacking. Of Mark's seventy-three words, thirty-one are identical to words in Matthew. This is 42.47 percent of Mark's word count, a higher than average correlation.[15] The number of differences is less great than in the other passages above, only fifty-one, or just 69.86 percent. But even such relatively less striking difference does not speak convincingly for literary dependence. Nor does the agreement require literary dependence as an explanation. Having looked closely at the actual data, we can only conclude that we are not at all dealing with a summary that shows literary dependence at all. We have before us rather various reports of events associated with the region of Gennesaret.

Verbal Agreements

Aren't there striking verbal agreements that cannot be explained except by literary dependence? Aren't such agreements clear proof of the use of literary sources? Decades ago John C. Hawkins compiled a formidable number of similar-appearing

15. On p. 128 we calculated the average agreement between Matthew and Mark at 40.99 percent.

formulations.[16] He argued that these "identities in language . . . are so numerous and close, and in many cases they contain constructions of words which are so very unusual or even peculiar, that the use of written Greek documents is prima facie suggested by them."[17]

Under close scrutiny, however, these turn out to furnish no proof for literary dependence among the Synoptic Gospels.

Alleged Agreement: A Second Look

Hawkins deals with individual passages, with verses or parts of verses that are plucked out of their contexts. When the entire pericopes are studied, an entirely different picture emerges. Let us examine two examples:

Consider, first, his comparison of Mark 15:10 with Matthew 27:18.[18] Five of the nine words in the Marcan verse are identical with Matthew. This is an agreement of 55.55 percent. Two more words share the same verbal stem.

Yet in the entire pericope, which in Mark consists of 104 words, there are only nine words that are fully identical in Matthew, Mark, and Luke—8.65 percent. This is considerably under the average agreement of 22.17 percent that we established on pages 127–29. Now Matthew and Mark share an additional thirty-three fully identical words, a total of forty-two or 40.39 percent agreement. This is very close to the normal percentage of agreement that we observed in previous chapters. On the other hand, Mark and Luke share only four additional identical words, for a total of thirteen or 12.5 percent agreement, far below the average of 34.29 percent.

The percentage of difference in wording lies considerably above the average (noted in parentheses; see p. 128): Matthew–Mark, 129 differences or 124.04 percent (95.68 percent); Mark–Luke, 144 differences or 138.46 percent (100.43 percent).

For a second example to show that the appearance of Hawkins' comparisons belies the reality, consider his comparison of Mark 5:8 with Luke 7:29.[19] The two verses share only the use of

---

16. *Horae Synopticae: Contributions to the Study of the Synoptic Problem*, 2d, rev. ed. (Oxford: Clarendon, 1909; repr. ed., Grand Rapids: Baker, 1968).

17. Ibid., 54.

18. Ibid., 56

19. Ibid.

γαρ (*gar*) to join a verb of speaking with the dative of the person addressed. In Mark this verb is linked with an imperative of direct address. In Luke this verb is linked, however, with an infinitive of indirect address. Of Mark's eleven words, three are fully identical with those in Luke, or 27.27 percent. Yet of the 326 words in the entire pericope, only forty-five are fully identical in Matthew, Mark, and Luke. This is no more than 13.8 percent (the average we established earlier was 22.17 percent).

Matthew and Mark have sixty-two fully identical words or 19.02 percent (we have suggested an overall average identity of 40.99 percent). This is less than half the average. Mark and Luke share 121 identical words or 37.12 percent, slightly higher than the overall average we have calculated (34.29 percent).

Differences for Mark and Matthew come to 305, or 93.56 percent, which is very near the average of 95.68 percent. For Mark and Luke they come to 277, or 84.97 percent, less than the average of 100.43 percent.

These two examples illustrate that the "identities in language" that Hawkins claims to show are less profound than they might appear at first glance.

Words of Jesus, the Septuagint, and Verbal Identity

But let us cast our net wider. Of the fifty-eight passages that Hawkins lists to show verbal identity between Mark and the other Synoptics,[20] only twenty deal with all three Synoptic Gospels. The rest show similarities in formulation between just two Synoptics. Thirty-two of the fifty-eight are words of Jesus. Nine passages cite statements made by other persons. One is an Old Testament quotation. In other words, in forty-two of the fifty-eight passages, the probability of agreement is much higher than average, since the Synoptics exhibit the highest level of agreement precisely when they quote Jesus' words or the Old Testament, as we have already observed.

In section B[21] Hawkins gives comparative statistics from the Greek Old Testament (the Septuagint, or LXX), which was the Bi-

20. Ibid., 54–63. There are fifty-nine examples in this section, but A.iv.1 on 57 shows similarity between Luke and Matthew, not Mark. Likewise, the eighteen examples on 63–65 also deal with similarities between Matthew and Luke. These are not evidence for, but rather against, the two-source theory.

21. Ibid., 57–63.

ble for much of the church during the time the Gospels were being written. Hawkins' own figures show that when the Synoptics
show similarity in individual words or short formulations, their
use often reflects that of the LXX.

For example, Hawkins lists similarities with LXX usage in
forty-five cases.[22] In eleven cases similarity is lacking, as Hawkins writes "never (or "not") in LXX." Six times a Synoptic formulation occurs once in the LXX. In two cases it is found twice in
the LXX and in two more cases four times. In one case Synoptic
usage is reflected four times in the LXX and in another five times.
Once Hawkins characterizes Synoptic usage as "rare" in relation
to the LXX. In all these cases, influence by the LXX can hardly
be regarded as demonstrable on the basis of comparative usage.

In the remaining twenty-one cases, however, the situation
changes. Influence by the LXX is quite possible. Hawkins lists
the number of occurrences of Synoptic usage once as "frequent"
and three times as "very frequent." Various other individual Synoptic expressions occur in the LXX seventy, thirty, twenty-two,
nineteen, eighteen, and fifteen times, respectively. One Synoptic
expression is found twelve times in the LXX, another ten times,
another nine times, and another eight times. Four Synoptic expressions occur seven times in the LXX and another six times.

Of the dozen Synoptic passages listed in this section of Hawkins' study that lack LXX parallels,[23] six relate Jesus' words and
two relate quotes from other persons (the Syrophoenecian
women, Mark 7:28; Hawkins, p. 60); those who rebuke the synagogue official (Mark 5:35; Hawkins, p. 63). This leaves just four
passages without plausible parallel elsewhere in either estab-

22. There are forty-seven passages listed in this section, but in two cases no
parallels with the LXX are cited. See examples B.ii.1 on 60 and B.ii.21 on 62.

23. Hawkins gives a total of fifteen such passages. Yet in two of these cases
he does cite a close parallel in the LXX; see B.i.11 on 58. and B.ii.22 on 62. And
in a third case he cites parallels from other Jewish and papyrological sources;
see B.ii.11 on 61. We also note that, while εἷς τις (see Mark 14:47; Hawkins,
B.iii.7, 63) has no LXX parallel, the use of εἷς as an article is very common in
the LXX and close to the usage in Mark 14:47. See Frederick C. Conybeare and
St. George Stock, *A Grammar of Septuagint Greek* (1905; reprint ed., Peabody,
Mass.: Hendrickson, 1988), 25f. In Hawkins, section B.ii.23 on 62, Mark 14:13
should be corrected to Mark 14:33. In the very next entry ματισμένον should be
corrected to ἱματισμένον.

lished LXX usage or in the words of Jesus or other persons (where the degree of similarity is normally quite high).

We conclude that, contrary to appearances, the "identities in language" listed by Hawkins furnish no proof of literary dependence among the Synoptic Gospels.

Unilinear Structure

The greatest problem that can be advanced to dispute a rejection of literary dependence is the unilinear structure that the three Synoptics have in common: in the beginning Galilee, in the middle the Transfiguration, at the end Jerusalem. While John reports three Jerusalem visits (2:13–25; 5:1–47; 7:1–10:39), the Synoptics know of only one. Isn't this classic Synoptic structure an indicator of literary dependence?

One must reckon with the fact that in the three years of Jesus' public ministry he could have been in Jerusalem as many as nine times. For he fulfilled the law with its command that every Jewish man appear before the Lord in Jerusalem three times annually. None of the Gospels mention these Jerusalem visits with anything approaching completeness. The authors were not biographers in the modern sense, registering every geographic movement in the course of a subject's life. The final Jerusalem visit, however, with its crucifixion and resurrection had to be mentioned by every Gospel without exception. But to do so they had no need to resort to a literary exemplar.

Peter's confession, Jesus' first passion prediction, and the transfiguration were far too significant to be passed over in silence.

Jesus' baptism was regarded generally as the beginning of his public ministry; that means that John the Baptist must also come into clear view. No literary exemplar would have been required to learn that Jesus' work began in Galilee, that he had called his first disciples there, or that his disciples became the first witnesses to his great miracles in that same locale.

Apart from such central facts, shared by all of the Synoptics, there is much that is not strictly uniform. Mark has no equivalent to the Sermon on the Mount; Luke lacks the material found in Mark 6:45–8:26; the structure of Luke 9:51–18:14 hardly compares to the other two Synoptics. Of the twenty-nine miracles mentioned in the Synoptics, just eleven are mentioned in all three. That is 37.93 percent, a good deal more than one-third—and to some extent they are variously placed in each respective Gospel. Of the forty parables, fully seven are found in all three Synoptics. Matthew and Luke have four in common. That accounts for eleven; the other twenty-nine are distributed as unique material among the three Synoptics: Matthew has eleven, Mark one, and Luke seventeen.

If one scrutinizes the material closely, one discovers that there is really not too much left in terms of similarity between the three Synoptic Gospels. Neither their so-called narrative order (*akoluthia*; see pp. 83–91) nor their general framework requires acceptance of the outlook that literary dependence is at work among them.

Having dealt with the first major question—whether it is really possible to understand the entire compass of the Synoptic data without accepting literary dependence—we now turn to a second issue, how the Synoptics may have come into being.

10

The Origin
of the Synoptic Gospels

How did the Synoptic Gospels come into existence if not through some form of mutual literary dependence? The answer to this question involves four stages: (1) tradition; (2) a forgotten factor; (3) the transition from memory to manuscript, and (4) the ancient testimony of Christians.

The Role of Tradition

Historical-critical theology assumes that a period of oral tradition preceded the formation of the written Gospels (see Fig. 10.1). During this period isolated words and stories were formed and refashioned. They took shape independently of each other, the theory goes, and were passed along individually. Ultimately they were grouped according to similar form, key word or theme, or other considerations. Evangelical scholars have often taken up this view of Gospel formation themselves (see Fig. 10.2), although with different motives than the advocates of historical-critical theology. Evangelicals usually value traditions as reliable historical material going back to Jesus, while historical-critical theologians usually see the creative early church as the originator, although they concede that a small amount of truly authentic material is preserved.

But, in any case, this phase of tradition formation separates what Jesus said and did from the Gospels themselves. According to this view, the Gospels are not in direct contact with Jesus himself but only directly relate to tradition. Since "tradition" is allegedly made up of isolated bits of material, any coherence among various accounts is chalked up to regular working of laws that govern how tradition forms or, more commonly, to a conscious creative effort on the part of each author. The historical-critical outlook declares part of the tradition to be legend or myth; this means that "tradition" is by no means reliable transmission of what Jesus said and did. It is rather simply a collective term referring to stories told about Jesus. Tradition is what purportedly circulated from and about Jesus.

In evangelical theology the counterclaim is advanced that the tradition behind the Gospels is reliable. This rules out thoughts of myth and legend. Evangelical scholars distinguish between the tradition and its literary reworking in the Gospels; they take heart because in their view historical tradition stands behind the Gospels. What they fail to see is that, without good warrant, they accept at face value the modern literary-critical (and in part also form-critical) hypotheses. They accept as a given the picture of individual, isolated bits of tradition because they wish to find firm historical footing in that tradition. But they fail to see that they thereby cooperate with historical-critical theology's attempt to sever a direct connection between Jesus and the Gospels by inserting the wedge of an anonymous tradition. Like historical-critical advocates, evangelicals often allow for "theologies" on the part of each Gospel writer as formative principles behind the Gospels they write. They fail to note that seeing the Gospels primarily as conscious human intellectual creations seriously weakens their status as clear eyewitness testimony of Jesus' words and works, described from each Gospel writer's perspective.

Historical-critical theology *must* posit different theologies for each Gospel writer. Otherwise it could not account for the discrepancy between the data in the Synoptic Gospels and its theories. Differences among the three Synoptics are inexplicable as mere stylistic improvements. Interpretation that does full justice to Scripture, however, finds this approach both unnecessary and inappropriate.

Figure 10.1. The Rise of the Gospels According to Historical-Critical Theory

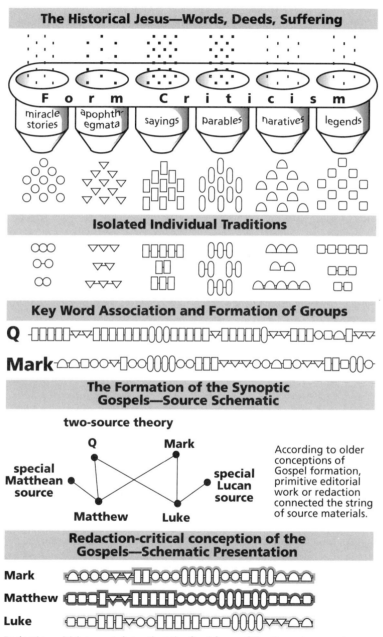

The Historical Jesus—Words, Deeds, Suffering

Form Criticism

miracle stories | apophthegmata | sayings | parables | naratives | legends

Isolated Individual Traditions

Key Word Association and Formation of Groups

Q

Mark

The Formation of the Synoptic Gospels—Source Schematic

two-source theory

Q　　Mark

special Matthean source

special Lucan source

Matthew　Luke

According to older conceptions of Gospel formation, primitive editorial work or redaction connected the string of source materials.

Redaction-critical conception of the Gospels—Schematic Presentation

Mark

Matthew

Luke

Redaction criticism postulates that the final form of the Gospels was set within the theology of each individual evangelist.

Figure 10.2. Evangelical Variations on the Historical-Critical Theory

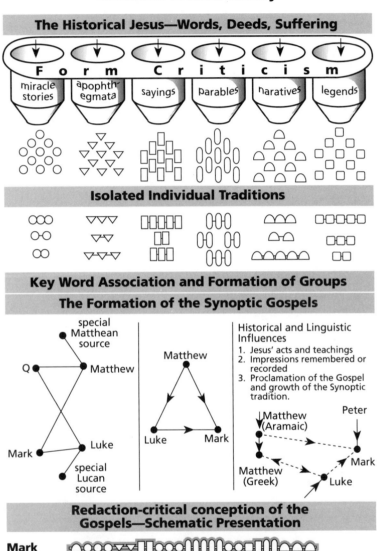

The Historical Jesus—Words, Deeds, Suffering

F o r m   C r i t i c i s m

miracle stories | apophthegmata | sayings | parables | narratives | legends

Isolated Individual Traditions

Key Word Association and Formation of Groups

The Formation of the Synoptic Gospels

special Matthean source

Q ● — ● Matthew

Mark ● — ● Luke

special Lucan source

Matthew
Luke   Mark

Historical and Linguistic Influences
1. Jesus' acts and teachings
2. Impressions remembered or recorded
3. Proclamation of the Gospel and growth of the Synoptic tradition.

Matthew (Aramaic)   Peter

Matthew (Greek)   Mark
Luke

Redaction-critical conception of the Gospels—Schematic Presentation

Mark

Matthew

Luke

Redaction criticism postulates that the final form of the Gospels was set within the theology of each individual evangelist.

180

Likely the transmission of what Jesus said and did played a vital role in early church teaching and missionary proclamation. But the needs of and use by the early church are not the source for the rise of the Gospel materials. What the Gospels record did not first pass through a "history of the Synoptic tradition."

The "history of the Synoptic tradition" is a fairy tale of criticism. Through the use of nineteenth-century literary criteria, that criticism explained the "setting of the life of Jesus" as a redactional invention. It atomized the Gospels' content into isolated traditions. It issued the prejudgment that the Gospel materials should be understood as "folk tradition," and it applied categories from the study of folk tales to these supposed isolated traditions, sorting them into the well-known form critical categories.

A "history of the Synoptic tradition" was created by comparing the various versions of the same pericope as it appeared in Matthew, Mark, and Luke. Since, according to the two-source theory, Mark was the oldest Gospel, the structure of the alleged earliest version was derived from Mark. To deal with exceptions to the rule, the oldest version was sometimes discovered instead in Matthew or Luke.

Based on the two-source theory, form criticism saw Matthew's and Luke's divergences from Mark as creative expansion that followed established laws regarding how traditions develop. Literary criticism saw the same divergences—again based on the two-source theory—as conscious editorial emendations and literary reshaping of the available material. Redaction criticism—again assuming the two-source theory—treated differences among the Synoptic Gospels as the result of conscious innovation, growing from the writers' theological motives.

Thus historical-critical theology performed an admirable feat: It spent the same coin three times, when one doubts it ever possessed negotiable currency in the first place. And its sleight-of-hand is grounded on a hypothesis with no basis in the data of the Gospels. Going back to our initial question, "What role did tradition play in the forming of the Gospels?" the answer now should be clear. There was no period of oral tradition that preceded the formation of the Gospels. Tradition, in the sense that is usually ascribed to it, cannot even be assumed to have occurred.

We now move to a second consideration regarding the larger question of how the three Synoptic Gospels came into existence, if not through some form of mutual literary dependence.

A Forgotten Factor

Wolfgang Schadewaldt rightly states:[1] "To the concept of oral tradition one must add another concept, or rather fact: *memory*. That is especially important in Mark, for which Peter's reminiscences formed the basis. Study of Homer and other Greek literature, e.g. Plato, indicates the significance of *mnema*, recollection: a secure, but not rigid, living presence of what was, of what was once heard, of what is faithfully and dynamically retained in a person's mind and heart." Schadewaldt cites an example from his own life, then continues: "Yet people treat the perhaps forty years that passed between Jesus' death and the completion of the Gospels as if it were 300. I keep hearing, 'In the course of tradition. . . .' The human brain is capable of bridging the span of years, as I have experienced in my own life."

A time span of forty years can easily be bridged by memory—in fact, it can reach far beyond just four decades, spanning an entire lifetime of seven, eight, or even more decades. When one bears this in mind, no room remains for "folk tradition" in the sense that it has often been applied to the pericopes of the Synoptic Gospels.

One could speak of "original tradition" as concerning something an eyewitness passes on. What someone relates that was heard from a direct eyewitness could be called "secondary tradition." In the case of the Gospels, *tradition* is nothing other than that which puts the reader of the Gospels in touch with what the eyewitnesses personally heard, saw, and passed on. One could perhaps differentiate between eyewitness accounts and secondary tradition originated by those who passed along what they heard from the direct eyewitnesses and original hearers. But perhaps *tradition* is a term that should be dropped entirely in relation to the Gospels, for tradition in the sense of imprecise hearsay, passed on from generation to generation, is ruled out on temporal grounds alone.

---

1. "Die Zuverlässigkeit der synoptischen Tradition ["The Reliability of the Synoptic Tradition"]," *Theologische Beiträge* 13 (1982): 220.

Memory includes a personal relationship and intensifies to the extent that this relationship has significance for the one who remembers. Things of little importance are readily forgotten; but we graphically recall something that engages the heart. Both the quantity and the quality of recollection depend on the personal relationship to what is remembered. Eyewitnesses to Jesus' words and deeds would be expected to possess graphic memories. They *remembered* what their Lord and Savior had said and done!

Intensity and thoroughness of memory also are conditioned by *activation*. Activation of memory occurs:

1. *through the desire to recall,* especially in connection with certain significant occasions or for other reasons;
2. *through exchange with others* who share the memory;
3. *through being queried* by those who do not share it, but who can participate in it as it is remembered and related, and
4. *through a willingness to relate* a memory, even when no one asks.

The presupposition of such activation of memory is that it has taken fixed verbal form. *Memory can be exchanged and passed along only if it has been verbally expressed.* That in no way requires that a certain fixed verbalization can never be varied. A memory that is not put into words easily dissipates and can certainly not endure any longer than the person who retains the memory.

Memory is personal; it is conditioned by the person doing the remembering. Even if eyewitnesses recollect the same thing and are therefore together on the main points, every individual will recall something different, at least to some degree. One will retain the big picture, another will give precise detail. Which details cling to the memory and which do not depend on what a person has an eye for. What escapes the notice of one person rivets the attention of the next.

Memory is conditioned by culture. The modern European, thoroughly conditioned by formal education, sets recollections in a temporal framework with adverbs and verb tenses. Geographical locations are named. But these characteristics are not universal throughout the world—as anyone knows if they work outside Western-influenced circles for an extended time. How much less may we assume the spatial and temporal framework as given for other eras! If a reminiscence lacks certain exact spatio-temporal qualifications, that does not necessarily mean it is imprecise. If geographical features (such as mountains or seashores) are not identified by name but can only be inferred from the context, we are not automatically permitted to declare an account unhistorical and regard the reference as secondary and redactional. *The question of whether a recollection is precise can only be answered from within the frame of reference of the originating cultural context.* To disqualify statements as uncritical or secondary because they do not correspond to the demands that one's own age and cultural circle sets for valid reports indicates deficient historical understanding and a dearth of anthropological insight.

This is not to suggest that there was no concern for accuracy as we know it in antiquity. Schadewaldt cites an example from early church history that illustrates a precision in recollection the permits no falsification:

> . . . in a sermon about the account of a lame man being lowered through the roof on a bed or pallet [Mark 2:4–9] . . . , the preacher substituted a more literary Greek word (*skimpous*) for the original word (*krabbotos*) used by Jesus in Mark's Gospel. Immediately one of his hearers called out: "Are you superior to the one who said *krabbotos*?" (The account is recorded in the ancient historian Sozomen I, 11; see *Migne's Patrology Gr.* LXVII col. 889) In any case, there was very strong control in this instance over the words Jesus used. That is how it most likely was from the beginning.[2]

If the words of a sermon were monitored with such care, how much more concern would have attended the linguistic fixing of the Gospels, so that all they report reflects just what took place? Fritz Reinecker gives us these thoughts:

> At the time the Gospels were written, the apostles and Jesus' brothers were still living. With consciousness of their responsibility and exemplary love for the truth, they will have strictly ensured that the material in the Gospels be passed along unadulterated. There can be no talk of myth, legend, and saga. Saga and legend arise only if the connection with the events is severed. Myth is even less likely to have been allowed into the

2. Ibid.

Gospel tradition than saga. What are myths? They are the recasting of ideas in history. The apostolate, Jesus' relatives, and the numerous eyewitnesses will have nipped in the bud any appearance of saga and myth that might have threatened to find a place in the four Gospels. For the same reasons we should resist the modern critical outlook that asserts that Jewish missionary theology, oriental mythology, or legends spun from the early church's faith forced their way into the disciples' accounts.[3]

Not "folk tradition" but the recollection of eyewitnesses is the foundation of the four New Testament Gospels.

From Memory to Manuscript

As we continue to explore how the Synoptic Gospels came into being, let us now directly take up the matter of *the formation of the Gospels*: Jesus words, deeds, and suffering were remembered by many. Some had heard or experienced only a small portion; others were witnesses of his words and deeds "beginning from John's baptism to the time when Jesus was taken up from us" (Acts 1:22). Twelve of this latter group, as witnesses of his resurrection, were explicitly authorized, being chosen "to occupy this ministry and apostleship" (Acts 1:25 NASB).

Relevant to the formation of the Gospels are all those witnesses who put their recollections into words, thus making them possible to pass along. Especially significant were those expressly authorized to devote themselves to "the ministry of the word" (Acts 6:4). Their utterances are central in the verbal formulation of recollections. Such utterances could be passed along orally or set down in writing. Both probably were part of the transmission of Jesus' words and deeds. That Jesus had disciples who were adept writers is beyond question. I leave open for now detailed discussion of whether, to what extent, and when they put into writing things said by Jesus; I also will not go into the question

---

3. Fritz Rienecker, *Das Evangelium des Matthäus*, Wuppertaler Studienbibel Reihe NT, 9th ed. (1977), 3–4. Rienecker's grouping of *myth*, *legend*, and *saga* is drawn from German linguistics. Higher criticism does not use the term *saga* and the definition of *myth* is far different. Rienecker's point is that invented stories couldn't have infiltrated the accounts, as the eyewitnesses and relatives of Jesus were still around.

of whether Jesus schooled his disciples in systematic memorization of his teaching.

Original Tradition

It is possible that Matthew made a written record of what Jesus said while he spoke, or in retrospect after his ascension. This does not mean that we must understand the Papias fragment (to which we will turn shortly) as speaking of *logia* in a narrow sense (e.g., as the saying source Q). It is also possible that John put sayings of Jesus into written form long before he produced the fourth Gospel. I do not wish, however, to commit myself firmly to such possibilities, for they cannot be proven.

Some of Jesus' eyewitnesses who formulated their recollections verbally and expressed them orally had only occasional opportunity to pass them along. Others, thrust into the ministry of proclamation, undoubtedly stated repeatedly the memories they had formulated verbally. This could be described as original or primary tradition, if one is reluctant to dispense entirely with the concept of tradition in this connection. Then there came a time when this primary tradition was put into to writing [*verschriftlicht wurde*]—an occurrence with which we have to reckon in the case of both Matthew and John. In putting their accounts into written form,[4] the authors may have incorporated material previously written—if it existed.

Secondary Tradition

Expression in written form [*Verschriftlichung*] could have taken place, therefore, as eyewitnesses themselves transformed what they remembered, which had been verbally formulated and used as original tradition in their own ministries, into writing. Likewise, what an eyewitness remembered and related could be written down by another person who set the eyewitness testimony

---

4. [Linnemann uses the word *Verschriftlichung*, a term from German linguistics. She explains this as "the transition of a communication into another aggregate form. An analogy is water becoming ice: they have the same chemical composition, yet different physical properties. *Verschriftlichung* is thus a relevant term in the above discussion, for it aptly describes the change that takes place in linguistic form (oral to written; or one written form to another) with no change in content (as linguists like Güttgemanns have shown)."]

down into writing. That is what happened with Mark's Gospel, as we shall see.

Gathered Corporate Recollections

Another possibility of transformation into writing involves the establishing of the corporate recollection of many witnesses. Their recollections, which were already verbally fixed, could be gathered systematically in order to be transformed into written form. Such witnesses could have retained recollections that had already gone through extensive dissemination, and they might also possess memories of what had been said only once or a few times. Here the movement toward overall comprehension and final written form does not stem directly from eyewitnesses but from the particular Gospel writer. This is the manner in which Luke's Gospel arose, according to Luke 1:1–4 (see Fig. 10.3).

The Testimony of the Fathers

Ancient church tradition makes its own statement about the formation of the Gospels, so we are not dependent on sheer speculation in this matter, nor are we restricted to the internal evidence of the Gospels. Reliable historical tradition does exist. The oldest reports we possess go back to the time of the apostles. Papias (ca. 98–117)[5] relates:

> And the Presbyter [the apostle John[6]] used to say this, "Mark became Peter's interpreter and wrote accurately all that he remembered, not, indeed, in order, of the things said or done by the Lord. For he had not heard the Lord, nor had he followed him, but later on, as I said, followed Peter, who used to give teaching as necessity demanded but not making, as it were, an arrangement of the Lord's oracles. Thus Mark did not err in writing things down just as he remembered them. He was concerned about one thing: not to leave out anything he had heard, nor to relate it falsely.[7]

This is what Papias was told regarding Mark. Papias goes on to say that "Matthew compiled the words in Hebrew dialect [the Ar-

5. See chapter 9, f.n. 12.
6. See T. Zahn, *Einleitung in das Neue Testament*, vol. 2 (Leipzig, 1899) 216–17.
7. Eusebius *Ecclesiastical History* 3.39.15–16.

Figure 10.3. The Rise of the Gospels from Memory to Manuscript

"The Holy Spirit . . . will . . . remind you of all that I have said to you" (John 14:26).
The starting point: Jesus' words, deeds, and suffering; events transpire and are remembered by many.

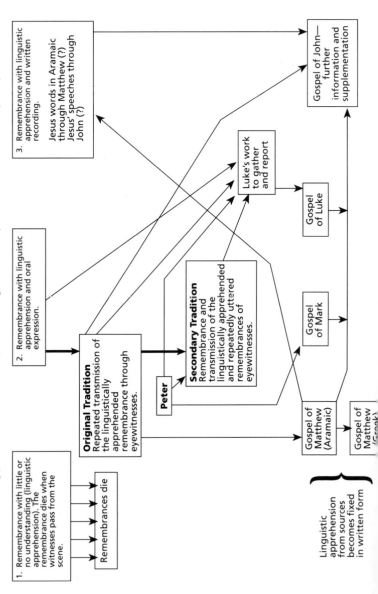

amaic language], which each person translated according to his own ability."[8]

From Irenaeus we learn that Matthew "compiled a written Gospel for use among the Jews and in their own language at the same time that Peter and Paul were in Rome, evangelizing and edifying[9] the church. After their death [literally *exodus*] Mark, the student and interpreter of Peter, also passed Peter's preaching along to us in writing, just as Luke, too, the companion of Paul, composed a book containing the Gospel Paul preached."[10]

These reports are as exact as we could possibly wish. Matthew's Gospel[11] was composed in Aramaic[12] by Matthew, Jesus' disciple (see Matthew 9:9[13]), at a time when both Paul and Peter were active in Rome. Paul is said to have lived there from the years 61 to 63 in his own residence. Thereafter he apparently was transferred into the praetorium (Phil. 1:13[14]) prior to execution by beheading in 64 (63, according to some). If Peter was active in

8. Ibid.

9. Gr. *themelioun*, literally "to lay a foundation." In the NT it is used only figuratively. Unless one prefers to find Irenaeus mistaken here, one must assume that he is reflecting NT usage.

10. Irenaeus *Adv. Haer.* 3.1.1; cf. Eusebius *Ecclesiastical History* 5.8.2–3.

11. τὰ λόγια, Papias' words for what Matthew writes here, are widely viewed as referring to his gospel in an Aramaic form. It is unjustified to insist on taking it overliterally, e.g. by restricting it to a sayings collection: Mark's gospel is said to consist of "what the Lord said and did" but is also said to pass along *logioi*. Both Irenaeus and other sources confirm this: cf. Zahn, *Einleitung*, vol. 2, 254–56 with note 4.

12. Cf. Zahn, *Einleitung*, vol. 2, 267ff.

13. Cf. Zahn, *Einleitung*, vol. 2, 258ff.

14. Paul's alleged trip to Spain most likely owes its origin to his travel plans attested only in Rom 15:24, along with the surprising conclusion of Acts (28:30–31.). The conclusion is, however, quite plausible if one supposes that Acts was written while Nero was still in power. During that time would it have been wise to write freely about the fire of Rome and the martyrdom of both renowned apostles? The political situation may well help explain how Paul and Peter—well known to each other and in Rome at the same time—seem not to have encountered each other. Paul was, after all, under supervision, and anyone contacting him would probably have been noted by the authorities. It may have been well advised for Peter not to have presented himself to these authorities on a platter, so to speak, and thus risk putting them on the trail of all the Christian communities in Rome. It is not necessary to invent a Pauline voyage to Spain in order to account for their apparent lack of contact with each other at that time.

Rome for just a year or even less[15] before he suffered martyrdom under Nero in 64 (as generally accepted), then the date for Matthew's Aramaic Gospel may be placed precisely at 63.

The formation of both Mark and Luke are related to the deaths of Peter and Paul. There is no compelling apparent reason for a long span of time to have passed. One can safely assume that these Gospels were written between 64 and 66. The most ancient Christian accounts leave no room, therefore, for the assumption that the Gospels were copied from each other. The time span between them is much too short to allow this. According to higher criticism at least ten years must be allowed to make the alleged literary dependence possible. That is all the more true in light of other ancient accounts that locate the origin of the Gospels in various locales: Matthew in Judea, Luke in Achaia, Mark in Rome.[16]

But doesn't Luke presuppose in his Prologue (Luke 1:1–4) that he knew of other Gospels that existed prior to his? By no means. Literally, Luke states that many had undertaken to develop a lengthy narration (description) of Jesus' life. There is no hint that such narration was extant in written form. To translate *anataxasthai* (from *anatassomai*, which the NIV translates "draw up") in Luke 1:1 as "write" or "compose" is misleading. Had Mark's or Matthew's Gospel lain before Luke as he wrote—which has already been shown to be impossible—then he surely would not have described the two of them as *many* (*polloi*). Nor can he have meant apocryphal Gospels, for they did not yet exist in the first century. Accordingly, Luke can only be speaking about extensive efforts to relate the words, deeds, and suffering of Christ as a whole, not in written but in oral form. A probable occasion for this would be the Gospel's spread to Gentiles, who had not had the opportunity to observe Jesus' earthly ministry. These converts would certainly have requested eyewitnesses who came their way to give them a coherent account of Jesus' deeds and teachings. One can imagine that during his travels with Paul Luke was often a witness of such spontaneous retelling; this may

15. Zahn, *Einleitung*, 2.19.

16. On Matthew see Zahn, *Einleitung*, 2.267–69; on Mark, see ibid., 215–16. That Luke arose in Achaia is attested twice in ancient gospel prologues; see Kurt Aland, *Synopsis Quattuor Evangeliorum*, 3d ed. (Stuttgart: 1965), 533, 539.

have kindled a desire in him to sift through everything carefully, as he says he did prior to writing (Luke 1:3).

The possibility for this arose when he came to Jerusalem with Paul at the end of the third missionary journey (cf. *we* in Acts 21:15), then remained in Judea until Paul's departure for Rome after his Caesarean imprisonment (note the *we* once more in Acts 27:1). This two-year period would have furnished sufficient time and opportunity to establish what eyewitnesses and servants of the word could pass along. After Paul's death he could have set to work writing without delay.

It is fair to conclude, then, that accounts from ancient Christian sources point to the rise of the three Synoptic Gospels during a span of three or four years, in three different locales separated from each other by hundreds of kilometers. This rules out a literary dependence. Nothing is to be found in the Gospels themselves that contradicts what these ancient sources affirm.

Part 4

Why Four Gospels?

11

The Purpose of the Four Gospels

What our Lord Jesus said, did, and suffered is found in four documents rather than one. This fact has called forth much criticism and doubt about the Gospels' inspiration. The basic argument runs: "Why should that which is, in a distinctive manner, the basis for our faith have been propagated in various versions, each independent of the others?"

There is, however, a clear intention behind the Gospels' fourfold form. *The intention involves the legal principle instituted by God*: ". . .on the evidence of two or three witnesses a matter shall be confirmed" (Deut. 19:15b NASB). God, who knows that we depend on the testimony of those who themselves saw and heard Jesus, made sure that the joyous message necessary for our salvation was transmitted to us not singly but multiply. *The independent witnesses confirm one another in complementary fashion.* See figures 11.1 to 11.6 below.

This intention to complement appears quite obvious to the unprejudiced reader, but it is unthinkable to a theology founded on the decree that the Gospels report unhistorical "testimonies of belief." This theology can only regard the content of the Gospels as stories invented by early believers to propagate Christian faith. As the historical information passed on by early church fathers disturbs the hypotheses of higher criticism, the fathers are rejected as being untrustworthy. Such a theology cannot progress beyond a question mark as to why we have the stories in four-fold form, "according to Matthew," "according to Mark," "according to Luke," and also "according to John."

Agreement among the Gospels extends far enough that one witness confirms the other as trustworthy. Based on that established trustworthiness, one can also accept the reliability of what alone one attests. "Historicizing" (that is, taking what the Gospels report at face value) is wrongly and contemptuously viewed as a methodological error by those who follow historical-critical theology. But just such confidence is appropriate to the object and a correct approach to the Gospels. This is not to suggest, of course, that the Gospels' message is exhaustively contained merely in the "historical" matter they report.

Every Gospel presents a complete, unique testimony. It owes its existence to direct or indirect eyewitnesses. In each testimony a distinctive personal individuality, and specific perspective takes written form. God did not extinguish the personal individuality of each Gospel writer[1] but rather made use of it, as it is written: "Men moved by the Holy Spirit spoke from God" (2 Pet. 1:21b NASB). In each of the four Gospels we can, therefore, discover a unique facet of the entirety of what took place, a true depiction of events that is recorded authoritatively and found nowhere else.

As the four testimonies supplement each other we arrive at the complete picture of what our Lord Jesus said, did, and suffered. This does not mean, of course, that we are to construct from the four one unitary harmony. At the level of individual pericopes, too, we gain a complete portrait of the event from that which the various Gospels report. This is not to be disparagingly condemned as "harmonizing"; it is, rather, the normal procedure of the historian who uses several reports of the same event. The question must be posed in each case, nevertheless, whether two or more Gospels cover an identical event or a similar occurrence, the same saying or variants of what was spoken in different situations. Here much work remains to be done, for we cannot employ the over-hasty identification common in historical-

1. I use *gospel writer* (*Evangelienschreiber*) advisedly, since the term *evangelist* (*Evangelist*), which is often used, has other connotions in our language, while the word *author* (*Verfasser*) leads to erroneous associations.

Figure 11.1.   Jesus' Life and Ministry—Unrecorded

Period of ministry activity: three years
3 x 365 days = 1095 days
Active ministry: about 1000 days

If Jesus spent an average . . .   His total time would have been . . .
  2 hours a day preaching   2000 hours
  2 hours a day instructing disciples   2000 hours
  1/2 hour working signs and wonders   500 hours

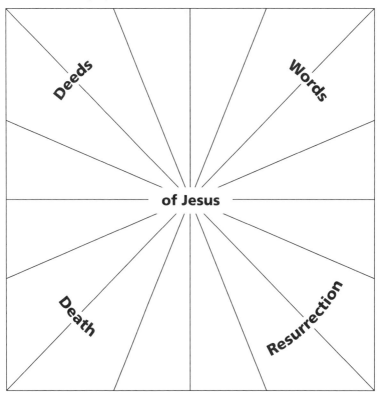

Jesus did many other things as well. If every one of them were
written down I suppose that even the whole world would not have
room for the books that would be written.
John 21:25

Figure 11.2. Jesus' Life and Ministry—
According to Matthew

Period of ministry activity: three years
3 x 365 days = 1095 days
Active ministry: about 1000 days

If Jesus spent an average . . .	His total time would have been . . .
2 hours a day preaching	2000 hours
2 hours a day instructing disciples	2000 hours
1/2 hour working signs and wonders	500 hours

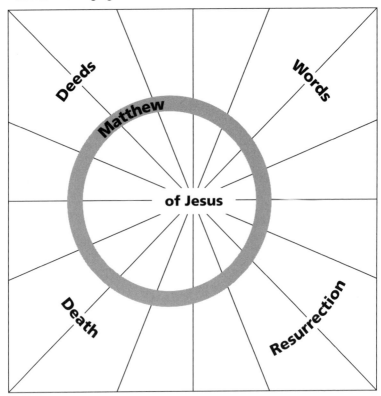

Jesus did many other things as well. If every one of them were
written down I suppose that even the whole world would not have
room for the books that would be written.
John 21:25

Figure 11.3.   Jesus' Life and Ministry—
According to Mark

Period of ministry activity: three years
3 x 365 days = 1095 days
Active ministry: about 1000 days

If Jesus spent an average . . .   His total time would have been . . .
  2 hours a day preaching   2000 hours
  2 hours a day instructing disciples   2000 hours
  1/2 hour working signs and wonders   500 hours

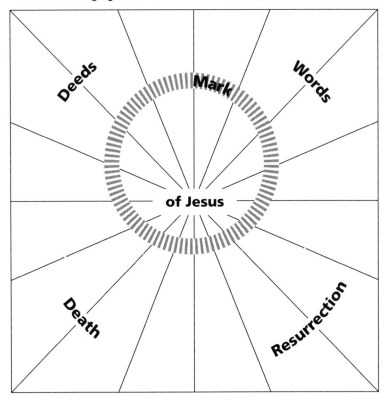

Jesus did many other things as well. If every one of them were
written down I suppose that even the whole world would not have
room for the books that would be written.
John 21:25

Figure 11.4.   Jesus' Life and Ministry—
According to Luke

Period of ministry activity: three years
3 x 365 days = 1095 days
Active ministry: about 1000 days

If Jesus spent an average . . .   His total time would have been . . .
   2 hours a day preaching   2000 hours
   2 hours a day instructing disciples   2000 hours
   1/2 hour working signs and wonders   500 hours

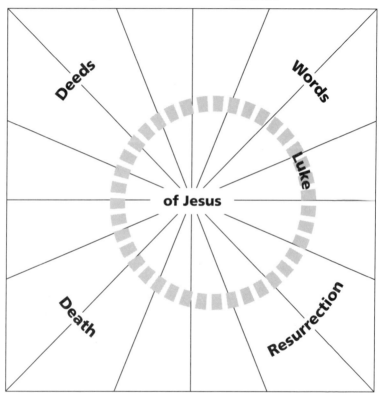

Jesus did many other things as well. If every one of them were
written down I suppose that even the whole world would not have
room for the books that would be written.
John 21:25

Figure 11.5. Jesus' Life and Ministry—
According to the Synoptics

Period of ministry activity: three years
3 x 365 days = 1095 days
Active ministry: about 1000 days

If Jesus spent an average . . .   His total time would have been . . .

  2 hours a day preaching   2000 hours
  2 hours a day instructing disciples   2000 hours
  1/2 hour working signs and wonders   500 hours

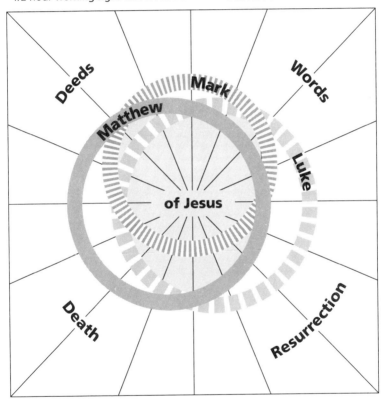

Jesus did many other things as well. If every one of them were
written down I suppose that even the whole world would not have
room for the books that would be written.
John 21:25

Shared material

Unshared material

Figure 11.6. Jesus' Life and Ministry— The Four-Fold Gospel

Period of ministry activity: three years
3 x 365 days = 1095 days
Active ministry: about 1000 days

If Jesus spent an average . . .   His total time would have been . . .
  2 hours a day preaching   2000 hours
  2 hours a day instructing disciples   2000 hours
  1/2 hour working signs and wonders   500 hours

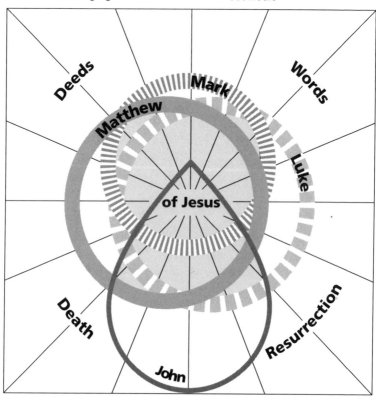

Jesus did many other things as well. If every one of them were written down I suppose that even the whole world would not have room for the books that would be written.
John 21:25

. . . men spoke from God as they were carried along by the Holy Spirit.
2 Peter 1:21

Shared material

Unshared material

critical exegesis, where reports with formally similar elements are treated as intentionally altered versions of just one event, or even a nonevent.

The respective versions of pericopes in the four Gospels do not only supplement each other; they also interpret each other complementarily. Where something is perhaps unresolved or unanswered in one, it is clarified by another.

Figures 11.1 through 11.6 illustrate how we may visualize this complementary and supplementary work of the Gospels.

12

The Treatment
of the Four Gospels

I hope chapter 11 made clear that it is permissible to interpret a pericope within the framework of one Gospel writer without scrutinizing its parallel pericopes in other Gospels. Every Gospel, in and by itself, presents a valid testimony. Further, it is possible to make a Synoptic comparison to highlight which features of a pericope are shared by various Gospels, which features are unique or shared by two Gospel writers, and how each writer fits into the common portrait. In this fashion a total picture of a pericope can emerge. See a sample of this in Fig. 12.1 below.

It is also possible, in principle, to recognize something of the perspective of the Gospel writer by studying individual pericopes. After a careful examination of an entire Gospel, conclusions that summarize the observations can be drawn. The result, however, does not comprise a *theology* of the Gospel writer. *Theology is the result of a conscious effort to arrive at one's own autonomous outlook.* It is the result of human mental maneuverings. The point-of-view of the eyewitnesses, in contrast, does not arise through the arbitrary effort of an individual; it is, rather, inherent in the unmistakable givenness of a person and his circumstances [*ist mit dem unverwechselbaren Sosein einer Person und mit ihren Umständen mitgegeben*]. The Holy Spirit uses a person and his or her individuality; it is not a matter of the person attempting to construct something peculiar.

If we have painstakingly determined that parallel passages really deal with the same event, but individual features still appear to contradict each other when the various reports are combined, we should not allow ourselves to fall into confusion. Perhaps we lack just that bit of information that would enable us to recognize how apparently contradictory data can be brought together. Perhaps we need to come up short at times to test whether we trust in God's word or our own cleverness. A good many things can be clarified if we ask the Lord in prayer for clarity.

In all essential respects, in any case, there is agreement; and every Gospels writer delivers an account complete in itself.

It remains for me only to thank the Lord, who in his great wisdom has committed to us the joyous message, trustworthily attested from four different quarters. The entire work of salvation, which our Lord Jesus Christ provided in words, actions, and suffering is transmitted to us reliably. There is no need for us to follow the "cleverly devised fables" (2 Pet. 1:16) of critical hypotheses that wither as soon as the light of truth shines on them.

Figure 12.1.   A Case Study: Supplementary Synoptic Comparison

Pericope: Jesus' baptism (Matt. 3:13–17; Mark 1:9–11; Luke 3:21–22. John offers no direct parallel. He reports what happened before and after the baptism but mentions Jesus' baptism only in retrospect. Thus John 1:29–34 is not included here.)

Shared Information-Matthew-Mark-Luke	Additional information
[Time reference]: at that time (Matt.), in those days (Mark)	When all the people were being baptized (Luke 3:21)
from Galilee (Matt. 3:19; Mark 1:9)	Jesus came from Nazareth (Mark 1:9)
Jesus was baptized (Matt. 3:16; Mark 1:9; Luke 3:21)	to the Jordan (Matt. 3:13)
he climbed out of the water (Matt. 3:16; Mark 1:9)	to John (Matt. 3:13)

heaven (the heavens) open(ed) (Matt. 3:16; Mark 1:10; Luke 3:21)	to let himself be baptized by him (Matt. 3:13)
and the Spirit (Matt. 3:16; Mark 1:10; Luke 3:21)	discussion between John and Jesus (Matt. 3:14–16)
descended (Matt. 3:16; Mark 1:10; Luke 3:21)	Jesus was baptized (Matt. 3:16; Mark 1:9; Luke 3:21)
like a dove (Matt. 3:16; Mark 1:10; Luke 3:21)	into the Jordan (Mark 1:9)
upon (Mark: into) him (Matt. 3:16; Mark 1:10; Luke 3:21)	by John (Mark 1:9)
and a voice out of (the) heaven(s) (Matt. 3:17; Mark 1:11; Luke 3:22)	as Jesus was praying (Luke 3:21)
occurred (Mark 1:11; Luke 3:22)	literally: the heavens were rent (Mark 1:10)
You are (Mark 1:11; Luke 3:22 [Jesus' own perspective; subjective])	of God (Matt. 3:16); Holy (Luke 3:22)
my beloved Son, in you (Mark 1:11; Luke 3:22) I take pleasure	he saw (Matt. 3:16)
	in bodily form (Luke 3:22)
	saying (Matt. 3:17)
	this is (Matt. 3:17; perspective of the Baptist, John 1:32; objective)
	in whom (Matt. 3:17)

Summary of the Information Presented

In those days (when [John the Baptist ministered and] all the people were being baptized), Jesus came from Nazareth in Galilee to the Jordan to John, in order to allow himself to be baptized by him. (John however rebuffed him and said: "I need to be baptized by you; and do you come to me?" But Jesus answered him and said, "Permit it at this time; for this is fitting to fulfill all righteousness.")
When Jesus had been baptized (in the Jordan) and came out of the water, the heaven(s) open(ed) (as Jesus prayed) and (he saw) the (Holy) Spirit (of God) descend (in bodily form) like a dove and come on (into) him.
And (behold) a voice out of (the) heaven(s) occurred (saying): "You are (This is my beloved son, in you (in whom) I take pleasure."

Epilog

By God's grace I have been able to show in this book that historical-critical theology's claim to be "science"—so spellbinding for so many—is unjustified.

With the evidence advanced I would like to throw open the door to freedom for those who have groped into a trap, urged along by the insistence that the results of this "science" cannot be circumvented, that it offers the only alternative to regression into the naive, intellectually infantile realm of a long-vanished precritical yesterday. My desire is to erect a warning sign: "Caution! Trap!" so others will not stumble into it, too.

This self-deluding philosophy does not deserve to be called science. No one need become subject to it. The prison door is open; the inmates can come out. But there is genuine freedom only in Jesus, in what he did on Golgotha to liberate us from sin and the power of the lie. It is not enough to repudiate historical-critical theology, as salutary and justified as that may be. Without him we are in danger of stepping right into the next trap we encounter.

It is not my intention to point fingers at advocates of historical-critical theology, though it has been necessary to mention a few of them by name. They are neither dumb nor incompetent; they are rather intelligent and respectable by human standards. Often they are even pious. But they are prisoners of a system. What happened to most of them continues to happen to many students today: They may be born again and want to serve the Lord by becoming pastors. Therefore they study theology. In Germany there are no accredited institutions of higher learning that uphold the trustworthiness of the Bible, so theological study descends inexorably into historical-critical theology, the trap of a pseudo-science that leads away from the faith.

Others have still never come to know Jesus personally as their Lord and Savior. As a rule, in fact, one seldom hears pastors proclaim any more that people are lost sinners who can be saved only if they turn to Christ. And no wonder: They have been required by church authorities to be schooled in historical-critical theology. As a result of this forced march through years of pseudo-scientific study, pastors usually lack all missionary or evangelistic competence. The same forced march was made, however, by the church authorities themselves years ago. The desolation is total and comprehensive.

But there is grace! There is redemption! A decisive conversion to Jesus breaks the bonds of historical-critical theology. And yet an end should be made to this forced march and its ensnaring termination. Yes, we need state- and church-accredited institutes of higher learning that give Scripture, and thereby Christ, the high place they deserve.

These closing words apply especially to the situation in Germany. For readers in Britain or America, where the situation with respect to Christian scholarship and education may not yet be quite so dire, may I urge that you preserve those colleges, seminaries, and other institutions that remain true. Watch over all the distinctives that make them strong in the faith which was once for all delivered (Jude 3).

You might need to change for refinement and growth—or mourning and repentance—but please change only out of obedience to Christ. Never allow changes simply because of pressure to keep up with "scientific" standards of the modern age that are not truly scientific, for they are not true when measured by the standard of God's word.

Be watchful and defend the holy faith that is once for all entrusted to the saints (Jude 3).

Bibliography

Aland, Kurt. *Synopsis Quattuor Evangeliorum*, 3d ed. Stuttgart: Deutsche Bibelstiftung, 1965.

Conzelmann, H. and Lindemann, A. *Arbeitsbuch zum Neuen Testament*, 5th ed. Tübingen, 1980.

Dürr, Günther. "J. M. Goeze—ein Kämpfer für die Wahrheit der Heiligen Schrift." *Bibel und Gemeinde*: 71, 97–105; 211–22; 301–12.

Farmer, W. R. "A 'Skeleton in the Closet' of Gospel Research." *Biblical Research* 6 (1961): 18–42.

_____. *The Synoptic Problem: A Critical Analysis*, rev. ed. Dillsboro, N.C.: Western North Carolina Press, 1976.

Haacker, Klaus. *Neutestamentliche Wissenschaft*. Wuppertal, 1981.

Hawkins, John C. *Horac Synopticae: Contributions to the Study of the Synoptic Problem*. 2d, rev. ed. Oxford: Clarendon, 1909; repr. ed., Grand Rapids: Baker, 1968.

Huck, Albert. *Deutsche Evangeliensynopse*, 3d ed. Tübingen, 1961.

Koester, H. *Introduction to the New Testament*, vol. 2: *History and Literature of Early Christianity*. Philadelphia: Fortress, 1982 (=*Einführung in das Neue Testament im Rahmen der Religionsgeschichte der hellenistisch-römischen Zeit.*, New York: 1980).

Külling, R. *Zur Datierung der 'Genesis-P-Stücke'*, 2d ed. Riehen, 1985.

Marxsen, W. *Einleitung in das Neue Testament*, 4th ed. Gütersloh, 1978.

Mauerhofer, Erich. "Die synoptische Frage." *Fundamentum* 2 (1982): 91–98; 3 (1982): 41–46; 4 (1982): 57–63; 1 (1983): 51–62.

Michel, Karl-Heinz. *Anfänge der Bibelkritik*. Wuppertal, 1985.

Morganthaler, R. *Statistitik des neutestamentlichen Wortschatzes*. Frankfurt: Gotthelf, 1958.

Rienecker, Fritz. *Das Evangelium des Matthäus*, 9th ed. Wuppertaler Studienbibel Reihe NT, 1977.

Riesner, Rainer. "Wie sicher ist die Zwei-Quellen-Theorie?" *Theologische Beiträge* 8.2 (1977): 49–73.

Schadewaldt, Wolfgang. "Die Zuverlässigkeit der synoptischen Tradition." *Theologische Beiträge* 13 (1982): 198–223.

Schweitzer, Albert. *The Quest of the Historical Jesus*. Trans. by W. Montgomery. London: A. and C. Black, 1948 (=*Von Reimarus zu Wrede*, 4th ed. Tübingen: 1926 [=2d ed., 1913]).

Spurgeon, Charles H. *Auf Dein Wort: Andachten für jeden Tag*, 2d ed. Bielefeld, 1986.

Stoldt, H. H. *History and Criticism of the Marcan Hypothesis*. Macon, Ga.: Mercer University Press, 1980.

Strecker, Georg, and Udo Schnelle. *Einführung in die neutestamentliche Exegese*, 2d ed. UTB 1252. Göttingen, 1985.

Stuhlhofer, Franz. *Jesus und seine Schüler: Wie zuverlässig wurden Jesu Worte überliefert?* Basel: Brunnen, 1991.

Watson, David C. C. *Fact or Fantasy? The Authenticity of the Gospels*. Worthing, England: J. E. Walter, 1980.

Yarbrough, Robert W. "The Date of Papias: A Reassessment." *Journal of the Evangelical Theological Society* 26.2 (1983): 181–91.

Zahn, T. *Einleitung in das Neue Testament*, Vol. 2. Leipzig, 1899.

Zimmermann, Heinrich. *Neutestamentliche Methodenlehre*, 7th ed. Rev. by Klaus Kliesch, 1982.

Index

Abbreviation by redactor, 104, 105, 106, 110, 132
Academic New Testament study, 43–66, 210
Achaia, 190
Acting agent, 160
Activation of memory, 183, 188
A.D. 35 source. *See* Aramaic lost gospels.
Additional minor details, 15, 55, 76, 99–108, 115–17, 147–48, 149, 150, 151
Agreement among Gospels. *See* Commonality.
Akoluthia, 48, 72, 83–91, 93, 176
Aland, Kurt, 71, 85, 86–91, 111
Anti-Christian bias, 20, 83–84, 159
Apothegmata, 179, 180
Aramaic gospel hypothesis. *See* Aramaic lost gospels.
Aramaic, language, 10, 30, 162–65, 187–89; lost gospels, 10, 26, 28–36, 39, 46, 49, 55–56, 68, 180
Arbeitsbuch zum Neuen Testament, Conzelmann and Lindemann, 59–62
Articles in vocabulary, 134
Ascension, 162, 185
Assertion, 22, 64–65
Augustine, 45
Authority of Jesus questioned, 124–25
Auxiliary verbs in vocabulary, 134
Bacon, Francis, 19
Baptism of Jesus, 113–18, 175, 206–7
Baur, Ferdinand Christian, 32–33

Beatitudes, 167
Betrayal and arrest of Jesus, 126
Biography, 84
Birth narratives, 38
Bultmann, Rudolf, 68, 84n
Call to discipleship, 122–23
Catch of fish, 169n
Chain of dependent hypotheses. *See* Circular logic.
Church tradition, 12, 28, 29, 30, 34, 37, 152, 158–59, 177–81, 187–91
Circular logic, 10, 11, 49, 58, 61, 68, 109
Cleansing of the temple, 124
Coin in the fish's mouth, 169n
Collections of writings, 10, 31, 32, 177
Commentaries, 12–13
Commonality, in material, 10, 14, 75–81, 147, 150–52, 156–58, 159, 161, 164, 165, 171–75, 201–2, 206; in narrative sequence, 71–72, 84–95, 159; in structure, 175, 176, 196
Communication, 83, 161–65, 179–80, 181, 185–91
Comparable material study, 156
Composite verbs, 53
Computer investigation, 13
Conception, 23–24
Conjunctions in vocabulary, 134
Conspectus locorum parallelorum evangeliorum, Aland, 85
Contradictions, apparent, 168
Conzelmann, H., 59–62
Copying, 146, 147
Course of event, 160, 161

Cross-section analysis, 14, 109–29, 149
Crucifixion. *See* Passion narratives.
Cultural framework of memory, 183–84
Curse on fig tree, 169n
Dating of Synoptics, 29, 30, 37–38, 64–65, 182, 183–84, 189–90
Deeds, communicating, 161
Dependence, 68–73; assumptions, 10–11, 37–38, 83, 92–94, 109–10, 111, 158; forms of, 14–15, 145–49; hypothesis, 10–15, 46, 47–56; in summary pericopes, 170–71; vocabulary and, 132–43; worldview of, 158–59
Deposit. *See* Linguistic deposit.
Desire to remember, 183
Destruction of temple foretold, 125
Deutero-Mark, 55–56
Deviation, extent of, 15, 102n, 103–8
Die Statistik des neutestamentlichen Wortschatzes, Morgenthaler, 71
Direct, communication, 28, 161, 163; dependence, 11
Discrepancies. *See* Deviation, extent of.
Documentary theories. *See* Source criticism; Two-source theory.
Dominical words. *See* Words and acts of Jesus.
Doublets, 167
Eichhorn, Johann Gottfried, 28–30, 46
Einleitung in das Neue Testament, Marxsen, 56–58
Encoding, linguistic, 161–62
Eusebius, 27, 32
Evangelicals, 72, 177–78, 180
Even vocabulary use, 135–39, 140
Events, 159–65; described, 83; remembered, 161–62, 177, 182–85, 188
Exemplar. *See* Source criticism.
Expansion by redactor, 11, 104, 105, 106, 132
Explanation of sower parable, 121
Eyewitness accounts, 12, 13, 14–15, 27, 29, 30, 37, 45, 57, 64, 83, 157, 161–63, 165, 167, 175, 178, 182–85, 186–91, 196
Factors of communication, 159–65

Falsification of hypothesis, 15, 60, 152, 157
Farmer, William R., 36, 39, 44
Fathers, testimony of, 187–91, 195
Faust, 106
Feeding, of the five thousand, 122, 169n; of the four thousand, 169n
First passion prediction, 122, 175
Fixing linguistic form, 160–65, 183, 187, 188
Folk tradition, Gospels as, 181, 182, 185
Form criticism, 10, 14, 47, 69, 119–27, 178, 179, 180, 181
Formation of Gospels. *See* Origin of Gospels.
Framework of event, 160, 161
Free reworking. *See* Redactional reworking.
Galilean ministry of Jesus, 175
Gathered corporate recollections, 187–88
Genealogies, 38, 76
Gentiles, witness to, 190
Germany, theological education in, 13, 210
Gieseler, Johann Karl Ludwig, 31
Goethe, 106
Goeze, J. M., 41, 42
Gospel of the Nazarenes. *See* Aramaic lost gospels.
Gospels, purpose of, 195–203
Graf, K. H., 21. *See also* Graf-Wellhausen theories.
Graf-Wellhausen theories, 13
Greek language, 30, 162–65, 182
Griesbach hypothesis, 39, 72, 102, 111, 147, 151–52
Griesbach, Johann J., 26, 27–28, 30, 32
Grotius, Hugo, 19
"Harmonizing," 196
Hawkins, John C., 171–75
Healing, of blind and dumb demonic, 169n; of blind Bartimaeus, 124, 169n; of blind man in Bethsaida, 169n; of crippled woman, 169n; of daughter of the Syro-Phoenician woman, 169n, 174; of deaf and dumb man, 169n; of demoniac in the synagogue, 169n; of dumb demoniac, 169n; of epileptic son, 169n; of Gerasene demoniac,

169n, of Jairus' daughter, 121–22, 169n; of lame man, 169n, 184; of leper, 118, 169n; of Malchus' ear, 169n; of man born blind, 169n; of man with dropsy, 169n; of man with withered hand, 120–21, 169n; of paralyzed man, 59, 120, 169n; of Peter's mother–in–law, 119–20, 169n; of son of a royal official, 169n; of synagogue leader, 169n; of ten lepers, 169n; of two blind men, 169n; of woman with hemorrhage, 121–22, 169n

Hebrew gospel. *See* Aramaic lost gospels.

Herder, Johann Gottfried von, 29, 30, 31

Higher criticism. *See* Historical-critical study.

Hilgenfeld, Adolf, 34

Historical Criticism of the Bible, Linnemann, 9

Historical narrative, 84, 92–94

Historical-critical study, argument for, 195; bias, 12, 20, 83–84, 159; history of, 19–42; methodology, 159, 178, 195, 196; theology behind, 9–15, 19–42, 46, 64, 71–72, 195, 210

"Historicizing," 159, 196

History and Criticism of the Marcan Hypothesis, Stoldt, 44, 48

"History of the Synoptic tradition," 181

History, concept of, 158–59

Hobbes, Thomas, 19

Holtzmann, Heinrich Julius, 35–36

Holy Spirit, 162, 163, 205–6

Hugh, Johann Leonhard, 30, 31

Hume, David, 19

Hypothesis, 10–13, 24, 25–42, 45–48, 59, 62, 65, 67, 68, 109, 181

Identical words, 59–62, 112–14, 119–27, 128, 129, 170–75. *See also* Vocabulary; Word.

Identities in language. *See* Identical words.

Improved source theories, 25–28, 52, 110, 178, 181

Indirect, communication, 28, 161, 163; dependence, 11; witness, 196

Inner connections of events, 160, 161

Interrogatives in vocabulary, 134

Introduction to New Testament Exegesis, Strecker and Schnelle, 44–56

Introduction to the New Testament, Koester, 62–63

Intuition, 21–24

Irenaeus, 189

James, apostle, 30

Jannes and Jambres, 42

Jerusalem, Jesus at, 175

Jesus, ascension of, 162, 185; at Jerusalem, 175; baptism of, 113–18, 175, 206–7; before Pilate, 127; Galilean ministry, 175; genealogies of, 38, 76; Gospel writers and, 162; "historical," 36; miracles of, 166, 167, 169, 175–76, 179, 180; parables of, 59, 61–62, 121, 125, 166, 167, 176, 179, 180; passion and resurrection of, 85, 91, 92, 94, 127, 149, 169, 175, 185; transfiguration of, 123, 175; words and acts of, 10, 14, 20, 27, 59–60, 85, 102, 106, 131, 137, 138–39, 140, 142, 147, 149, 158–70, 173–75, 178, 179–80, 181–91, 195–202

John, apostle, 30, 187

John the Baptist, 122, 142, 175

John, origin of, 186, 188

Judas' agreement to betray Jesus, 126

Judea, 175, 190

Kant, Immanuel, 19

Käsemann, Ernst, 84n

Koester, Helmut, 62–63

Koine. *See* Greek.

Külling, Samuel R., 21–23

Lachmann, Karl, 10, 48, 56–57

Language, original Gospel, 30, 162–65, 187–89

Lavater, 40

Law, books of the. *See* Pentateuch.

Legend, 178, 179, 180, 184

Lessing, Gotthold Ephraim, 12, 26–27, 28–30, 31, 40–42, 46

Lindemann, A., 59–62

Linguistic, analysis, 14, 69–72, 76, 110, 115–17, 119–28; deposit, 131, 161, 163; fixing of an event, 160–65, 183, 187, 188; form, 99, 101, 111, 115; record, 162, 163; structure of event, 160; structures, 163–64; study, 156

Literary, assumptions, 10–11, 83, 92–94; criticism, 9–15, 19–42, 46, 159,

195, 196; parallels, 103–6, 112, 113, 135–36, 137, 138–39, 140, 141–42, 143; prototypes, 63; relationship, 109–10. *See also* Dependence.

Little children blessed, 123–24

Logienquelle source. *See* Q source.

Longitudinal analysis, 72, 131–43

Lost gospels. *See* Aramaic lost gospels.

Luke; additional minor details, 99–108, 115–17, 147–52; *akoluthia*, 88–90; and Q, 64–65; as source gospel, 10, 11, 15, 32, 33, 101, 181; commonality, 10, 77, 78–79, 80, 81, 88–91, 92, 93–94, 109–10, 149, 171–75; differences, 119–29, 131, 132, 147; formation of, 10–15, 34, 35, 37–38, 69, 72, 147; Griesbach hypothesis, 147; miracle accounts, 167; narrative sequence, 149; origin of, 26–36, 48, 49, 56, 69, 148, 151, 187, 188, 189, 190–91; parables, 166; parallel pericopes, 72, 76, 97–99, 102–8, 109–27, 169n, 170–71, 195–203; parallel words, 112–13; prologue, 190–91; record of Jesus' acts, 200; summaries in, 170–71; unique material, 76–81; vocabulary of, 109–10, 131–35, 138–39, 140–43, 147, 162–63, 165

Marcan priority. *See* Mark, as source gospel.

Mark, 44; additional minor details, 99–108, 115–17, 147–52; *akoluthia*, 84, 86–91; Aramaic, 162; as source gospel, 10, 11, 15, 28, 30–31, 32, 33, 38, 48–62, 64–65, 99–102, 103–6, 109–10, 111, 114, 131, 132, 147, 179, 180, 181; commonalities, 14, 77, 80, 81, 84–94, 109–10, 150, 171–75, 188; cross-section investigation, 119–27; formation of, 10–15, 34, 37–38, 55–56, 69; Greek, 162–63; Griesbach hypothesis, 147; in Matthew-Luke conflict, 32–33; miracle accounts, 167; narrative sequence, 149; origin of, 26–36, 54, 55–56, 147, 148, 152, 168, 182, 186, 187, 188, 189, 190; parables, 166; parallel pericopes, 14, 76, 97–108, 109–27, 169n, 170–71, 195–203; record of Jesus'

acts, 199; summaries in, 170–71; unique material, 97, 107; vocabulary, 52, 53, 72, 112–14, 131–35, 137–43, 147; *Vorlage*, 37

Marxsen, Willi, 56–58

Matthew, 44; additional minor details, 99–108, 115–17, 147–52; *akoluthia*, 84–85, 86–88; and Q, 64–65; Aramaic, 162, 180, 187–89; as source gospel, 26–28, 30–31, 34–35, 48, 101, 151, 181; commonalities, 77, 78–79, 80, 81, 86–88, 91–94, 109–10, 149, 171–75; differences, 49, 119–29, 131, 132, 147; formation of, 10–15, 32, 33, 36, 37–38, 56, 69, 148, 186, 187–89; Greek, 162–63, 164–65, 180; Griesbach hypothesis, 147; Judaistic, 32–33; miracle accounts, 167, 175; narrative sequence, 149; origin of, 26–36, 56, 147, 151, 152, 189; parables, 166; parallel pericopes, 59, 72, 76, 97–108, 109–29, 169n, 170–71, 195–203; place written, 190; record of Jesus' acts, 198; summaries in, 170–71; unique material, 76–81; vocabulary of, 53, 72, 109–10, 131–35, 138–43, 147

Medical reports, 157

Mendelssohn, Moses, 40

Method, research, 67, 71–72, 75, 109–11, 115; theological science, 22–40, 43, 158–59, 195

Ministry of Jesus, 197–202

Miracle accounts, 166, 167, 169, 175–76, 179, 180, 197–202

Mnema. See Recollection in Gospel formation.

Monistic worldview, 158–59

Morgenthaler, Robert, 44, 71, 81, 132, 135n

Moses, 42

Multiple-source hypotheses, 39. *See also* Two-source hypothesis.

Myth, 178, 184–85

Narrative, fragments, 32, 33; hypothesis, 46–47; sequence, 48, 72, 83–95, 147, 149, 176

Nathan the Wise, Lessing, 26–27

Nero, 189n, 190

Neutestamentliche Methodenlehre, Zimmermann, 63–66

New hypotheses regarding the gospel writers seen as merely human history writers, Lessing, 26–27
New Testament criticism. *See* Historical critical study.
North America, theological education in, 210
Numbers, use of, 134
Old Testament, 13, 21–23, 102, 137, 138–39, 140, 142, 159, 165, 173–75
On the Dating of the 'P' Source in Genesis, Külling, 21
Oral tradition, 10, 25, 26, 29, 31, 35, 47, 68, 69, 177, 190, 191
Origins, Gospel, 10–15, 25–42, 48, 49, 54–56, 63–65, 69, 63–65, 69, 145–52, 155–91, 168
P source, 21, 22–23
Papias, 32, 168, 187–89
Parables, 166, 176, 179, 180; of great banquet, 167; of mustard seed, 59, 61–62; of royal wedding, 167; of sower, 121; of vineyard and tenants, 125
Parallel, pericopes, 14, 50–52, 59–60, 72, 76, 84–95, 97–108, 109–29, 149, 157n, 159, 165–70, 195–203, 206–7; words, 103–4, 112–17, 119–29, 132–43, 149–52
Participants in the event, 162
Passion narratives, 85, 91, 92, 94, 127, 149, 169, 175
Paul, apostle, 36, 41, 189, 190, 191
Pauline-Judaistic source conflict, 32–34
Paying taxes to Caesar, 123
Pentateuch, 13, 21
Pericopes, sequence of. *See* Parallel pericopes.
Perspectives of Gospel writers, 205
Peter, apostle, 29, 30, 35, 162, 168, 182, 187, 188, 189, 190; catch of fish, 169n; confession, 120, 175
Philosophy, 19–20, 209
Plagiarism, 146, 148
Plato, 182
Plot to kill Jesus, 126
Plucking grain on the Sabbath, 120
Positivistic philosophy, 157n
Précis, 146, 147
Precision of memory, 183–84
Preparation for Passover, 126

Prepositions in vocabulary, 134
Priestly writing, 21
Proclamation, early, 179, 180, 181
Prolegomena to the History of Ancient Israel, Wellhausen, 22–23
Prologue to Luke, 190–91
Pronouns in vocabulary, 134
Proof, scientific, 22, 64
Proper names in vocabulary, 140, 142
Prophets, books of the, 21
Proto-gospels. *See* Aramaic lost gospels.
Psalms, 21
Purpose of the parable, 121
Q source, 25, 26, 31–32, 33, 38, 57, 64–65, 76, 179, 180, 186
Quantitative analysis, 71–72, 109–29
Quotation, 146, 147
Raising, of Lazarus, 169n; of widow's son, 169n
Recollection in Gospel formation, 160–62; 177, 182–185, 188. *See also* Eyewitness accounts.
Redaction criticism, 10–15, 37, 69, 179, 180, 181
Redactional reworking, 11, 37, 104, 105, 132, 146, 147, 148–49, 150–51, 178, 181
Reflective citations, 102
Reimarus fragments, 27
Reimarus, Hermann, 19
Reinecker, Fritz, 184–85
Remembered event, 161–62
Research, 45, 71–73
Resurrection narratives, 85, 91, 92, 94, 127, 149, 169, 175, 185
Retold stories, 156–57
Reuss, E., 21
Riesner, Rainer, 35–36, 39
Ritschl, Albrecht, 34
Rome, 190–91
Sachordnung, 165n, 167
Saga, 184–85
Salvation in Christ, 206, 210
Sayings source. *See* Q source.
Sayings. *See* Words and acts of Jesus.
Schadewaldt, Wolfgang, 182, 184
Schenkel, D., 35–36
Schleiermacher, Friedrich, 31–32, 50
Schnelle, Udo, 44–56
Schweitzer, Albert, 35–36
Science, theology as. *See* Historical-critical study.

Scripture. *See* Word of God
Second passion prediction, 124
Secondary tradition, 64–65, 182, 186–
    87, 188; witnesses, 37
Semler, Johann, 19
Sentence structure, 14, 25
Septuagint, 165, 173–75
Sequence of pericopes, 165, 168–70
Sermon, by the Sea, 166; on the
    Mount, 76, 167, 175; on the Plain,
    76, 167
Seven forms of dependence, 145–49
Shared material, 201, 205
Smoothing, 11, 52, 55–56
Socio-cultural context, 156, 161–62,
    183–84
Source criticism, 10–15, 25–39, 46,
    131, 158–59. *See also* Two-source
    theory.
Sowing and harvest parables, 166
Spinoza, Benedict, 19
Stages of tradition formation, 64–66
*Statistik des Neutestamentlichen
    Wortschatzes*, Morgenthaler, 44
Stereotypical usage, 156, 161n, 162
Stilling of the storm, 169n
Stoldt, Hans-Herbert, 44, 48–50, 53–
    54, 84–85, 99–100
Storr, Gottlob Christian, 28, 29, 30
Strecker, Georg, 44–56
Structure of Synoptics, 165, 175–76
Symbols, 161–65
Synopsis Quattuor Evangeliorum,
    Aland, 71, 85n, 111
Synoptic Gospels, completeness of
    coverage, 168–69; construction,
    165, 175–76; dating of, 189–90;
    historical sequence, 92–94; narra-
    tive sequence in, 83–95; only liter-
    ature, 158; origins, 10–15, 25–42,
    63–65, 145–52, 155–91; parallel-
    ism in, 11, 97–108; problems,
    165–76; record of Jesus' acts, 198;
    sequence, 165, 168–70; structure
    of, 175–76; summaries, 70–71,
    165; topical arrangement, 165,
    166–67; variant readings, 161,
    165, 167–68; verbal agreements,
    165, 171–75; vocabulary, 11, 14,
    54; writers of, 178–81, 185–91
Synoptic problem, definition of, 10,
    44, 68; history of, 19–42, 45–46,
    67

Tendentious ideological/theological
    reworking, 146, 148
Tendenz criticism, 32–34
Testimony, of Church fathers, 177,
    187–91; of four Gospels, 195; va-
    lidity of, 205
Testing of hypotheses, 45, 59–62, 67
*The Synoptic Problem: A Critical Analy-
    sis*, Farmer, 44
Theological science. *See* Historical-
    critical study.
Theology of Gospel writers, 178–81,
    205
Theory, 21–25, 39
Thesis, 47
Third missionary journey of Paul, 191
Third passion prediction, 124
Tindal, Matthew, 19
Toland, John, 19
Topical arrangement of Synoptics,
    165, 166–67
Totally identical words. *See* Identical
    words.
Tradition, formation, 64–66, 177–78,
    179, 180, 181; history, 48, 54–56,
    64–66, 69; hypothesis, 46, 47;
    original, 170, 186, 188; secondary,
    64–65, 167, 182, 186–87, 188;
    stages of, 64–66; theories, 23–39
Transfiguration, 123, 175
Translation, 27
Transmission of words. *See* Commu-
    nication.
Triumphal entry, 124
Two-source theory, 11, 13, 25, 47, 54,
    57–58, 69, 136, 148, 151–52, 179,
    180, 181; assumptions, 37–39, 72,
    102, 111; opposition to, 41–42, 44;
    History of, 32–36
Unilinear Structure, 175–76
Unique material, 25, 26, 75–77, 79,
    80, 81
Unshared material, 201, 205
Ur-gospels. *See* Aramaic lost gospels.
Variants, 161, 165, 167–68
Verification, 60, 152, 157
Vocabulary, agreement, 10, 11, 14,
    53, 72, 109–10, 131–43, 147, 156–
    58, 171–75; even usage, 135–39; in
    common use, 161, 165; New Tes-
    tament, 134–35, 137, 140, 143;
    structure, 162, 163. *See also* Identi-
    cal words.

Walking on the water, 169n
Warning of persecution, 125–26
Wedding at Cana, 169n
Weiß, Bernhard, 34
Weiße, Christian H., 32, 33, 48, 49–50
Weizsäcker, K. H., 35–36
Wellhausen, Julius, 22–23. *See also* Graf-Wellhausen theory.
Who is the greatest? 123
Wilke, Christian Gottlob, 32, 33, 48–50
Word of God, 11, 14, 15, 19, 20, 42, 73, 158–59, 206

Word, as linguistic unit, 111, 115, 160–63; counts, 53, 54, 59, 62, 71–72, 77–81, 98, 100, 102–8, 119–29, 137–43, 147, 150, 151–52; order, 11, 158. *See also* Identical words; Vocabulary.
Words and acts of Jesus, 10, 14, 20, 27, 59–60, 85, 102, 106, 131, 137, 138–39, 140, 142, 147, 149, 158–70, 173–75, 178, 179–80, 181–91, 195–202
Worldview, 158–59
Written tradition, 25, 32, 69, 186, 188
Zimmermann, Heinrich, 63–66